FIRE AX
'STOP' MESSAGE

TAKE A RIDE WITH THE FIRE BRIGADE

by
Richard J. Small.
Post Grad Dip 1996 in Training
UK Fire Engineering Diploma 1981
Further and Adult Education Teacher's Cert 1993
BTEC Fire command/management studies 1999
NEBOSH National General Certificate 1997
(Grad IFE and Chartered MIPD until retirement)
And simply loads of other stuff.

Published by
Goodness Me Publishing Limited
www.goodnessmepublishing.co.uk

1

Is any of it true?
Well, yes, most of this book is born of a reality, mine, and probably that of many others. I have chosen not to identify people, with suitably respectful exceptions where applicable.

Protecting the innocent and guilty alike, this is a hopefully cathartic book of short anecdotes and stories. I have attempted to tell the truth from the humorous to downright tragic. The way it really was. Well, as I saw it anyway. If it looks like I believed some officers had their brains removed on promotion, I'm sorry, but it seemed that way to me.

**

**

If you spot any obviously intentional errors,
then well done,
but I'm afraid there's no prize.

**

Your choice -
You enter a smoke logged building on fire, you locate a family group of three people, a dear young child about 5, a young man about 23 and an elderly lady about 60, who reminds you of your grandmother.

You can only take one of them.

Who will you leave behind? The choice is yours, and yours alone. Make the wrong one and lose all three. It happens.

(The young man has the greatest chance of survival.
you must abandon the others to their own nightmares,
then learn to live with yours.)

**

'And now the doleful, dreadful, hideous Note
Of FIRE, is screem'd out with
a deep-strain'd throat;
Horror, and fear, and sad distracted Cryes,
Chide Sloth away, and bids the Sluggard rise;
Most direful Exclamations are let fly
From every Tongue, Tears stand in every Eye.'

Samuel Wiseman,
on the great fire of London

**

There exists in a good firefighter's soul, a spirit equal
to that of any fire they will meet.

Always aspire to emulate the most respected firefighter
on the watch, not the one they trust least.

'They who only walk on sunny days never
complete their journey.'
Vietnamese proverb.

Who might have an interest in this book?

Well, me first of course, after that, any firefighter past or present, or indeed a relative of one. For within these reminiscences and stories, they will undoubtedly find themselves intrigued by reminders of their own experiences, and for a moment they will be young and strong again. For those interested in life in the fire service, mostly as it was before it became a predominantly rescue service, they will find the simple truth. Anyone that likes a nose into other people's lives and a bit of gossip will also be mollified.

**

(If images are fairly rare, it's because we were too busy doing other things.)
**

Dedicated - to the dedicated themselves, past and present, and may I be forgiven for the many and oft foolish mistakes I made, trying to be that way.

Written with Jocey and Sam in mind.

Contents

(Not in chronological order – by any stretch of the imagination. Like my mind – a jumble.)

8

Life is neither film nor game. When trapped in a life-threatening situation, your part is not played by a stuntman and the director is never going to shout, 'cut, that's a wrap!' You will know despair and feel fear. Even the unbelievers will call to god for help. The pain will persist long after the rescue services finally find you and arrive. If you live, your memories will haunt you for a lifetime. The dead do not get up and have a cup of tea backstage. The curtain is final. Too many people cannot discern between digital imagery and reality.

Please, don't be one of them.

**

Signing up to serve.

It wasn't just a job, it was a duty, though I didn't fully realise the full implications immediately I joined. I was previously working as a technical assistant in a research laboratory in 1974 and the wages weren't enough for the mortgage and my young family. We'd buy a chicken (capon) and make it last four days between us, and our only useable heating source was an old paraffin fire. I saw an advert in the paper, 'Firemen Wanted', and showed it to my boss, 'look,' I said, 'I can find a job anywhere that pays more than here.' They couldn't help, so my fate was sealed. My studies towards Licentiate of the Royal Institute of Chemistry at an untimely end.

I applied to Northamptonshire County Fire Service who were recruiting to cater for the working week dropping from 56 hours to 48. At the interview, they unusually decided on the spot to offer me the job subject to medical. A medical that insisted on 20/20 vision, the same for fighter pilots. They needed 30 years out of you without glasses and no colour blindness.

(Years later I was to work with someone who had dangerous red/green colour blindness and whose doctor must have done what Nelson did with his telescope at Trafalgar. Good job he wasn't in bomb disposal!)

I was pleased with the opportunity to take more money home for my family but strangely it had not occurred to me that it was only more money because instead of a 36-hour week I would be doing 48 hours on shifts, nights and weekends and risking my life in the process. No wonder it was more money. Alternating night and day shift work is the worst of all systems for your health. Firefighters of forty, fifty or more years ago had a lower life expectancy than the general public, heart problems being high on the list of health problems. Hence, in part, why they retired at fifty-five years of age. They were running out of time and ability to sustain instant response to hard labour. The loud bells did nothing to calm the racing heart that only moments before was at peace. The adrenalin coursing through their veins did nothing but damage.

**

The medical.

I was using a 500cc twin Triumph motorcycle for transport at the time. First of the 'unit constructions', it had distributor ignition. If you know anything about such systems, you will know that water can easily affect the running. The evening of the medical, you've guessed, it was chucking it down with rain. Wearing heavy rubberised canvas waterproofs, (old and second hand when I was given them) I rode to my doctor's surgery in town. I waited until nearly time for the appointment and made myself known. 'Ah,' they said, 'we don't do them here, you need the brigade doctor in the next town.' They gave me an address and I left in a suitable hurry. The rain was quite heavy by now and I'm sure you know what Murphy's Law was about to bring my way. The engine faltered and stopped. I jumped off and had to push the heavy bike all the way to the docs. By the time I arrived, I was sweating like a pig, heart rate through the roof and almost exhausted – but – I still passed the medical. It must have been an omen. (Or they were really desperate.) Fate.

Brigade stores – the kitting out.
The brigade was run on a shoestring, though stores probably had none of them left either, or if they did, it was on its own. I was issued with two pairs of Melton wool fire trousers, at least four sizes too big .... but that is all they had left, so they were mine. Two fire tunics, one of which could have

passed for Victorian. Three shirts with detachable collars and a set of studs to hold them together, a pair of lace up black shoes, some black socks and a tie. A pair of rubber boots, a black helmet, a pair of debris gloves ... the plastichrome type, only for turning over debris after the fire had been tackled with <u>definitely no gloves</u>. If the debris was hot, the plastic melted. I recall at a later date having a hole in one glove and reported it to the station officer. He said, 'that's okay, I have a hole in one of mine, I will put in an order for stores.' And so, he did, and I did get a new glove .... that's right, he gave me his old, good glove, which was fortunately the correct hand, and he kept the new pair for himself. He who had no use for debris gloves. We were also issued with a scarf and an Acme thunderer evacuation whistle. Oh, and a pencil, which was marked with your brigade number and must never be lost. It was only exchanged for a new one when the stub was too small to hold.

Officers were obviously held in high esteem, because I recall receiving a stores delivery at station once, that had several rolls of cheap toilet paper and two luxurious, soft rolls ... they were marked, 'officers only'.

The brigade didn't even have its own dedicated radio scheme. It was shared with the police, and they had priority. In order to speak to fire control, we had to request access. 'NG NG message for NO, etc'

**

*Miner's intrinsic safety lamp, personal issue axe,
evacuation whistle, neck silk, a remnant of breathing
apparatus guideline.*
*It was also wise to carry a knife, pencil, and paper.
(For relaying messages without forgetting what was
said and in severe cases asking an officer to put in
writing what you might consider dangerous or illegal.)*

**

Journey to the first 'shout'.

Leicester Central Fire Station – training school

We'd been to training school, me and Bob. Ten weeks away from home, running about, lifting things and being shouted at. Sounds almost like a remedial centre, doesn't it, but it all took place at Leicester Central Fire Station and had the highest of motives, that is, service to others in distress from fire. Along with lots of shouting and running we had squad drill, ladder drill, pumping drill, first aid, (featuring a monotone Doctor who specialised in after lunch hypnotic sleep trances), knot tying, hose running, (good for taking spare skin off thumb knuckles and straining your back), and lectures on how to deal with what pleasures and horrors we might find out there in the 'real' world.

As it turned out, the 'real' world also consisted of running about, being shouted at and either painting or cleaning something.

We'd never seen a fire but were taught about them, just like we'd never seen a horse but were told how easy it was to rescue a frenzied and uncooperative bronco from its burning stables;

simply shove your thumb and finger up its nostrils, grip firmly and then lead it out like a lamb; needless to say, they did not demonstrate this. We'd never been on a roof either but just in case we did in the real world, and we slipped down a frosty roof towards an imminent death, we were instructed on two simple and fool proof methods; (What's that you say? 'Hang on to the guttering like in the movies'. No, neither of the options offered involved guttering ... except as a passing reference!) First method, on discovering that gravity had a good grip on you and was speeding you earthward down a sloping roof, just spread-eagle your body and relax. Apparently this gives maximum friction, and you will slow up – eventually. I guess the body might be a little reluctant to comply with the counter intuitive command of 'relax' under the circumstances and the mind may well be a touch concerned about the word 'eagle' being in the instructions. Strikes me it has certain connotations.

Version two was my favourite, if the lesser of two evils can be favourite, it was a less passive acceptance of what will be will be and consisted of taking your personal issue fireman's axe and driving the pointed end hard through the slates and hanging on to it like a climber in the crevasse would with his ice axe.

Though version two was favourite, it required the axe to be in hand all the time – if it wasn't, by the time you'd found the awkward axe pouch clasp and drawn the axe you'd be past any gutter hanging stage and into free flight, then you'd know

17

how the soaring eagle felt – for a short time anyway, then you'd know how a dead one felt.

We learned how to hold and direct jets of water at the right things – that is fires, and definitely not other people's eyeballs, - but not all fires, oh no, not that easy; fires involving flammable liquids, oils, metals like magnesium, molten cyanide and nitrate baths, glowing red cast iron, acetylene cylinders, (more of which later), hot walls, and electrical equipment – sometimes regardless of the power being off, these were all taboo, 'must nots'. We were taught where and how to attack the fire. The subject required that our neuron was fully engaged as it could result in a life-or-death event, so, no room for mistakes, or we'd be tackling chimney fires for the devil next.

One sunny morning, we were taken out for a special treat, down to secluded countryside, (so as not to frighten the public and embarrass the instructors no doubt) where we could set our big pumps into 'open water', the river. We were under one of those big electricity pylons; you know the sort, the ones with barbed wire all around the base and a big sign saying, 'Danger of Death, Keep Away, 120,000 volts.' One of my fellow recruits took hold of a jet and stood firm and determined as the high-pressure water surged from the hose at about half a ton a minute and he directed it straight at the high voltage power cables high above him, if he wasn't careful he could be joining them!
I said, 'Oi, they told us not to get electrical stuff wet.' His answer, steeped in recent and in-depth quality fire brigade training, moulded

18

around some sort of latent death wish, came back with smug confidence, 'Don't be daft; it rains on them all the time!'

I wonder where he is today, he certainly was confident, even if it be misplaced, and a self-confessed expert in many matters, but that's another story.

The wardens, I mean instructors, tortured us, I mean nurtured us, to overcome our burgeoning mixture of fears and blissful ignorance.

I recall one such shining example of a cultured and sensitive approach to our learning in particular. Again, it was a sunny July morning, and we were in the drill yard below the tower, a big one it was, 100 feet, that's thirty metres in new money. Halfway up, or down, depending on your perspective and which way you were travelling, was a large unglazed window opening, through which hose or casualties could be hauled or lowered.

On this occasion, part of the crew were to haul aloft a line of hose using a 'rope' which we had to call 'lines' unless we wanted punishing. On the order, 'knock off and make up' it was evident that the special knots that were needed in specific places and in a particular order for the event to occur as per the Drill Book, weren't, and didn't. Faces appeared at the window and hose was haphazardly lowered, but it didn't get far before the error of their ways was as evident to them as it was to all of us looking up; the hose was hauled aloft again, and the faces disappeared. After some while, the now agitated faces appeared once more, leaned out and the hose was lowered earthwards only to result in a tangle that had shortened the line – the hose and faces disappeared yet again, accompanied by the visible twitching of our instructor. At last, after what seemed about an hour, the hose was on its way down again, the even more flustered faces watched its decent to just over halfway .... then they ran out of line. At least they used their initiative this time; they strained out as far as they could and let the line go from the very ends of their fingertips.

Before the expensive hose, branch and line had hit the floor our instructor had thrown his cap to the ground and punched the side of the fire engine. Sadly, he seemed somewhat unimpressed with the hose drill and, obviously fearing we might let ourselves down with other equipment, he kindly re-arranged the afternoon sessions so that we could brush up on our ladder skills.

We spent the rest of the entire day running around the yard carrying heavy ladders and shouting ... and no tea break either, such was his concern for our wellbeing. They mercilessly taught us how to tie knots; all manner of knots for all manner of purpose; watching the instructor was like watching a magician, a deft sleight of hand and a beautiful, purposeful knot appeared before our eyes .... But how had he done it? That was the question. Different instructors had different ways of tying the same knot .... just a different magician with a variant on the same trick ...... more confusion. Once having made a reasonable shape from the line (rope) that somehow resembled the specimen-perfect example that the instructor held out proudly in front of him, it was time for us to move on ... now the knot had to be applied to the purpose, e.g., hose would be hauled aloft with a clove hitch first followed by a rolling hitch. Ok, so now we're on a bit of a roll and guess what, they expected us to be able to tie them behind our backs ..... and, in the dark ... where incidentally most of us had been from day one anyway! They don't do some of these knots today, they have specialist gear, but back then it was expected that we improvised with the minimum of equipment ... which, incidentally, was fortunate, as it was exactly what the Fire Brigade had on offer.

One of the great knots groups was the rescue knots; used to haul an unconscious body to or from aloft; if they weren't unconscious at the beginning they soon would be. These knots were, chair knot, bowline on the bight and my favourite the non-listed French bowline; all of these could be made into two big loops that could form a rudimentary 'parachute' harness that kept the body vertical.

As the end of the course drew near, a group of us were practicing our knots expertise in the old garages, which also doubled as sleeping quarters for a handful of unfortunates and was to be found in the far corner of the drill yard by the dustbins. Remember the chap who pointed water at the electrics? One recruit tied a large chair knot, and two others helped our friend to step each leg into separate loops, the loops were crossed, and an arm threaded through each upper loop; the knot was adjusted so as to be behind the neck (to support the head of the unconscious). Ok, all looked good, then, before he could extricate himself from the knot, it was suggested we try it out. Recruit Fireman instantly became recruit Guinea Pig as the group executed an experiment into the 'real world'. Immediately there was general agreement, and, like some Wild West lynch mob, the loose end of the 'rope' was thrown enthusiastically up and over a metal roof beam and, as if by magic, even more enthusiastic hands appeared and hauled the screaming 'guinea pig' up into the roof. Why was he screaming you ask, was he afraid of heights? No, it was all to do with the rope that went between his legs. It was pulled tight into his groin and allowed him the dubious pleasure of taking his entire body weight on his private bits. Rescue knot – cobblers – it was more like a medieval torture. Grimacing with enthusiastic fervour he swung painstakingly for a couple of minutes while the laughing subsided enough for the crew to regain sufficient composure and be able to lower him down.

Well, I've digressed far too much, but hope that you now have a flavour of the nature of some of our training. The gap between what we were taught and what we were expected to meet in the nasty real world was vast, cosmically vast.

One of our more serious lectures was on acetylene gas; highly flammable, explosive gas. Acetylene cylinders .... Even worse. 'Why?' you ask. They mustn't get too hot, they could explode, sending metal shrapnel in all directions and a great ball of burning hot gas into the surroundings, they mustn't be dropped, or they may explode as well, they apparently can explode with a heavy blow from a hammer. I wonder who they got to try that out? 'Oi, Malcolm fetch that 'ammer over 'ere.' If they are involved in fire they must be cooled .... But not with an actual jet of water .. oh no ... this could cause metal distortion and guess what? Yup, you're right, it could explode. Firemen, in those days were expected to pick up this unexploded and temperamental bomb and put it in a bath of cool water. The bath? You had to make your own bath out of ladders, canvas sheets and our faithful friend – rope.

Bob and I were posted to the same, quiet, station, that had few 'shouts' (calls for assistance), not to be confused with shouting, of which there was much, and we'd settled into our cleaning everything and being shouted at, practicing with equipment – and more shouting, being tested on our topography (knowledge of town streets etc) and being shouted at. On reflection that could be why I'm nearly deaf now.

Such was our journey to the first shout; we were to find the journey to the incident itself much shorter, quicker and with a somewhat different feel to it.

One day the bells went down, and we put on our boots, leggings and tunics and climbed aboard the big red engine, just the two of us learners in the back and our truly heroic leading fireman sat in the officer's seat and Ed the driver took us off down the road ahead, blue lights and two tones and all. Our officer turned to see 'his crew', his heart must have sunk, poor man.

'*Workshops fire …. Acetylene cylinder involved ….*' he warned us, and turned back to look at the oncoming road ahead.

Bob and I looked across the cab at each other as we hurtled faster and faster through the town to what could, by all the gruesome accounts of our old instructors, be an early death, we each gave a knowing look that said something like, 'well, they taught us how dangerous these cylinders were, they didn't even show us one, let alone let us practice with a dummy one; why doesn't the driver slow down and let it explode before we arrive; will we let our guvner down, does he really think we know what we are doing; will we be going home tonight or be scattered over Northamptonshire.' The looks spoke volumes, we understood it all; and then we too, turned to look at the oncoming road ahead. Such was the journey to our first shout into the real world.

In memory of my pal, the late Bob Childs, who died in a motorcycle accident some thirty years or so after joining the Northamptonshire Fire Service.

**

It was a two-year probation period and four years before becoming a qualified fireman. All the time in awe of longer serving and experienced firemen, and forever seeking the knowledge that, you too, could survive each new event.

**

Rushden

Rushden Fire Station
Built in 1902 after a tragic town fire. When I was
stationed there, the watch room was to the left of the
pillar, with the stairs to its right. The right hand (rear)
wall had been taken down and a flat roof extension put
on to accommodate modern petrol engine appliances.

Station personnel, ready to assist in a charity scooter
push. This appliance was travelling with the four-man
scooter, Dover to Edinburgh as I recall. You can see the
wheeled escape ladder on board, fifty feet extension and

moved around on carriage wheels by a crew of four. Quite exciting when you were working the moving spokes with your bare hands.

If they had said, 'You can sleep under the stairs and we'll give you free dinners,' then I'd gladly have done the job for nothing, such was my interest. At the start, anyway.

**

Arson - allegedly

A sixth sense kicks in when attending set fires, (arson), as it does when children have been involved. It's like a voice that whispers inside your head. Somehow you know. Intuition is rarely wrong. But can you prove it? Ah well. Sometimes, but it wasn't our job at the time. We just put them out.

There's always the odd give away, like the bloke who took his dog with him for a day out to the seaside – the only time ever to do so – and, oh dear, his pub caught fire while he was away. Or, the repair garage fire, totally gutted. Surprise,

surprise, everyone who had work done, still received their bill, how lucky that none of the paperwork was lost in the fire. The picture above is of a derelict factory. It has to be said, it was in better nick before the fire though. The previous week there had been a call to a small fire on the premises – it's what you might call 'seed corn'. The following week the place was well alight by the time we arrived. It was a Sunday if I recall, and the owner had been seen earlier that morning visiting his factory. More coincidences eh?   We were hampered at that job by poor water supplies, they were only two-inch mains with poor flow. The pump operator had to fill his tank and then pressurise the hose, there not being sufficient pressure and flow to sustain a working jet direct from the water main itself. The fire was burning on all floors and in danger of cutting off our firemen working inside.

Today, nobody would be sent into a job like that. They were back then.

Strange isn't it, back then we were forbidden to wear gloves at a fire. Today it is seen as vital.

Years later, as a station officer, I attended a fire in Huntingdon. It was a restaurant with a number of unfurnished rooms above. It was a devilishly hot fire on the first floor and a real struggle for the BA crews to get in and stay in, however, they succeeded in knocking the fire down, even though at some point, roof tiles were breaking around us below. Once the smoke had cleared, it was evidently an attempt at arson. The window which had been removed, had been taken out from the inside. In places where the fire had been prevented from spreading, the floor was covered in scrunched up newspaper. A pistol was found in one room, and we asked the police to check it out. It proved to be a replica. It was a good job well done by a hardworking and professional crew and the police had ample evidence of an inside attempt to destroy the property.

My favourite bit was being invited back to the station for a bacon sandwich. Preferable to going home to an empty house.

I am grateful for the memory.

Thank you, Andy.

**

Every so often a proper working job would replace the routine of false alarms, chip pans and chimney fires.

Ben and the drought of 1976.

It was 1976, and summer, and what a summer. The drought having started in September of 1975, had dragged its rainless days and nights inexorably nearly all the way to the September of 1976 when the heavens made up for it.... Big time. The drought was serious, crops failed, fires burned, reservoirs ran close to dry, in the old flooded valley reservoirs the once flooded roads became accessible again, the clay bed of the Thames was cracking, standpipes were in the streets as water supplies were cut off to houses, in Wales, water was turned off between seven at night and eight in the morning, an Emergency Drought Bill was rushed through Parliament, no cars were washed, no gardens watered, except with washing up water from the kitchen, even if you had water in a rain butt it wasn't yours to use, everyone looked for a spare house brick to put in the toilet cistern, flushing was only to be done when absolutely necessary, baths were rare and, almost by order, shallow, rivers ran low, some even disappeared altogether and canals were closed. In the southwest they went forty-five days without rain, elsewhere temperatures reached a daily thirty-two degrees centigrade for fifteen consecutive days .... it was hot ..... and from near the end of June 1976 it didn't change for months.

Plenty of fires mind you, despite most people taking events very seriously, even down to vigilante women patrolling golf clubs at night to ensure they weren't being watered, there were still the odd foolish ones whose discarded cigarettes ignited roadside verges, or the thrill seeker, dull of wit, that set fires deliberately.

Firemen ... there were no women in the Fire Brigade as it was called then, had to fight fires ... notably hot in their own right, I think you'll agree, ... in the merciless heat of the summer, wearing their shirt and trousers uniform under their fire kit. Imagine, middle of the day, not a cloud in sight, wearing waterproofs over woollen fire trousers, heavy rubber boots with steel plates in the soles, thick buttoned up to the neck heat loving black fire tunic and heavy cork helmet and then running about under the Sun in burning fields with beaters ... short lengths of canvas hose fixed to wooden handles, ... you see we didn't have much water either and fires aren't always in convenient places for fire engines.

I recall we attended a railway track fire in a remote area, after a long walk from the roadway we beat and stamped out the burning dried vegetation, but not so easy were the tar-soaked wooden sleepers that burned between the rails... using an old fireman's trick we turned to our emergency water supply .... carried conveniently in the bladder .... good job a train didn't come along otherwise they might have thought it some strange masonic ritual as we circled the steaming embers, with our leggings by our knees.

We were issued with two pairs of trousers, mine were several sizes too big, as I have already said, that was all stores had, mind you after 3 months they kindly did ask a seamstress to take 4 inches out of the waist for me ... she altered nothing else - only the waist size... three shirts, with detachable collars which my wife helpfully sewed on for me, and two fire tunics, it wasn't long before they were all soaked in sweat and the only solution was to wear them, waiting for them to dry out, often this was only at meal breaks .... By the time dinner was over, your shirt would be dry and ready for you to go out and do factory inspections or the like. You must by now have some idea of our fire clothing ... soaked in sweat or not, well I missed a bit of kit issue out ... and I still have the original issued from 1974, ... a 'neck silk' they called it, but it was made of cotton and like a large thin oblong scarf. The idea was to wrap it around your neck to fill the gap left by the tunic collar ... saved all sorts of horrible things going down the neck ! Sparks, burning embers, debris, rain, anything really; you could also wear it across the face ... a bit like a bank robber, now it kept out different things .... things that floated in the air like smoke smuts .. or things that flew in the air, like little black beetles attracted to our yellow helmets and leggings, or greenfly ... of which there was an unprecedented plague, I lived in hope it would keep out smoke too ... but I suspect that was wishful thinking on my part.

On the day of which I wish to write, we went to a twelve-pump fire at a burning forest in Northamptonshire, there were five of us on our fire appliance as we called them ... Fire Engines to everyone else ... as our driver negotiated the forest tracks, under the guidance of our leading fireman, Ben, we could feel the heat through the windows even from a distance. It was our third call-out of the day and, as ours was a normally quiet station, I couldn't help excitedly telling this to a fireman from another station; 'Oh, really?' he replied, 'this is our fifteenth.'

'Oh,' I thought, in subdued and silent reply.

After the requisite numbers of hours trying to make fire breaks and watching trees burn we were mobilised back to station as it was coming to the end of our shift. Normally we would just hang up our kit and go home, but this night ... perhaps we were officially entitled to a meal or something ... we were all asked, 'everyone for fish and chips?' 'Yes please,' came the chorus except for one, it was our long serving Leading Fireman Ben, 'I'll have a meat pie instead,' he called. A decision that might haunt his dreams later ... that's if he was to get any.

For myself there were to be no dreams and no sleep, I responded to the rapid beep of my station alerter (pager) for another call-out at about 11 pm.... and it was back to that damned forest again; this time an all-night vigil with another pump crew. We had a new, god fearing and upwardly mobile officer with us this time and his plan ..... no, not to let us take turns to sleep ... was to patrol the forest with buckets of water looking for hot spots. We did this from midnight till about eight am when we were allowed back to station .. and for me straight back on to the day shift .... thirty-six hours working with no sleep. True, they sent me home for a wash, breakfast and some clean clothes .... 'but don't be long!' shouted the officer as I cycled away from the station.

So, it was a couple of days before I was on duty with Ben again and my first chance to hear of his meat pie and its disturbing and resolute vengeance.

Government advice had flooded the media ... the only floods we had .... about not flushing toilets unless absolutely necessary ... everybody knew, and most had a house brick in the cistern to reduce volume. Nights were dry and airless, if you slept under anything it was just a sheet, windows were all open, inviting a reluctant air circulation to visit the home. Anyone caught wasting water was not only an enemy of the state but of the people ... who were getting tetchier as the hot days and hot nights wore on inexorably.

It was a small town and people like Ben were well known by many, he was a part of the community, respected for his service, an upholder of fine ideals and rules, a man of dignity with a reputation to be admired and kept.

On the 'night of the meat pie', Ben's neighbour's two sons, about eleven and twelve I'd guess, were camping in a tent in their back garden. They knew all about the drought and the rules; their father had taught them well.

It seems highly likely that the meat pie was having a serious argument with Ben's digestive system, the argument turned into a battle and then a war, a war that would last all night. Tortured mentally and physically, Ben was forced by nature's course ... or should that be curse .. to visit the toilet several times during the night. Every time he sat there in his misery his thoughts and ears would be filled with the voices of two boys in the next garden shouting, 'dad, dad, mister Thornley is flushing the toilet again!' As he sat in his alimentary misery the boy's voices would echo in his mind ... as if it wasn't bad enough.

Even if the neighbourhood was once asleep they certainly weren't as the chorus from inside the tent continued through the night and the open windows, 'dad, dad, he's still doing it, dad, he's flushing the toilet again!'

At least they'd heeded Government advice to heart, God bless them ...... not sure that's what Ben thought at the time mind you.

A memory from 1976 and the drought year
**

These were the days when the fire brigade put out the fire then put out the rubbish, everything was taken outside, the plaster off the walls shovelled out and the floor, what was left of it, swept clean. No doubt today, everything is left in situ for the investigation, and cleaning up is someone else's job.

Photo source unknown.
Rushden's drill and hose drying tower, built 1902.

The crew here are wearing black leg slip waterproofs. When I joined, we still had black helmets but had yellow waterproof over trousers. The crew here have pitched the 50 ft wheeled escape ladder, which in the very early days of the station would have been wheeled by hand around the town.

**

During my time at Rushden, I learned how to polish brass, clean the toilets and know my place. Rudimentary cooking lessons included, making pastry cleans your fingernails, and chopping caterpillar riddled cabbage finely means the men won't notice when it's cooked. I learned to keep my mouth shut when the home office inspector paid a visit and asked me questions, and that my station officer was best pleased when he could smell lots of disinfectant being used in the toilet cleaning. We did lots of good work for the community – for free! It was like a social service back then, for example, a lady needed her husband's bed moving downstairs due to an illness. The local football club needed a bulb changing on the flood lights, that involved a three-man drill on a four-man ladder. It was a quiet station with few shouts (emergency calls). It was so quiet, one Sunday a squirrel called in , wandered around the appliance bay, then left because it was bored. The station was nucleus manned. In other words, each weekday two groups would be on duty, so the appliance was fully manned. On nights and weekends only one group attended, and a turn out relied upon retained firemen turning in on their alerter. We had two appliances, a water tender and a water tender ladder. We had very little in the way of rescue kit.

I was blessed by having an amazing mentor in Eddie Hitcham and to whom I remain indebted for many aspects of my own career. A good fireman who walked to work with pride. (Wicked sense of humour mind.)

Political correctness hadn't been invented back then. I was asked by another fireman, where a particular street was. I didn't know. His response was, 'well you are no use to us then.' He meant it too. I bought a town map and cycled the streets to learn what I could. No sat nav back then either.

You could tune in your home radio to listen to the police or fire service back then. It wasn't illegal to do so, only if you acted on the information. It was always interesting to listen to various stations attending incidents .... any big fire could mean our station was also required. Time to get the bicycle ready.

The bicycle was already old, it was a gift from someone who no longer used it. I painted it red and did a few repairs. My station officer accused me of stealing paint from the fire brigade but apologised when I took the empty 'cherry red' tin in to show him. It was a colour I'd used on a motorcycle a few years before. Once, when pedalling like mad and answering the call to station, one of the pedals snapped off. Fate kindly intervened and I didn't fall off. I had the pedal welded back on by Ben of the pie; waste not want not.

Rushden had a long history of the leather trade and shoe making, there were many old buildings with oil-soaked wooden floors and benches. They burned well when involved in fire, but our biggest risk by far was a factory that made polyurethane foam. Raw materials like Toluene Diisocyanate were stored in bulk and when heated gave off cyanide gas. It was the main reason positive pressure breathing apparatus was introduced – to stop the gas being drawn into the mask on the in breath. Even experienced miner's canaries were no match for this stuff.

**

Petroleum inspections.
Some of us were trained to inspect fuel installations. Hose in good repair, vent pipes right height and condition, extinguisher etc. I was diligent but made a couple of mistakes. An old chap in a rural location ran a carpentry business and had his own petrol tank and pump. He was a nice old guy and all he needed was to put a lick of paint on the vent pipe and some other minor thing. I was supposed to write him a warning letter, but he seemed a decent chap and promised he would do these things before next week. Well, he didn't. Now I was in a mess of my own making. My station officer would want to know why there was a week delay in writing and why three visits had to be made. That nice old chap cost many others a bit of goodwill, but I don't suppose he cared.

Many farms had their own fuel stores too. On one inspection, the farmer called me in to his office and told me off. 'Why do you come here when we are busy with harvest or other seasonal matters. Why can't you turn up when we have time for you?'

I thought, 'he's quite right, we should.' I agreed with him, and he said with a sigh, 'come on then, I'll show you where the pumps are.'

In a cobbled courtyard, on all sides bounded by stone buildings and with gate access in two places, were the pumps. As we looked over the gate together, he said, 'I'll leave it with you then.'

As he left, I stared at the bull in the yard, between me and the pumps, the bull stared back, he seemed to be taking an overt interest in my shiny buttons and clip board and was returning my stare with interest. I decided I could inspect the pump from a distance and filled in the paperwork. With luck, the bull would be in place for all future inspectors. While I was learning the craft, I went with my station officer to inspect fuel pumps at another farm. The elderly farmer was a really good man, all he wanted to do was farm. He had no interest or skills in the bureaucratic new world in which he found himself embroiled. His son dealt with that for him. As we walked back to the car he said, 'of course, the old fuel tank is still under the floor in that barn.' A deathly hush followed. I suspect that had I not been there, the station officer would have said, 'if I were you, I'd keep quiet about that.' Sadly, the poor old farmer was now facing the expense of the tank being cleaned and filled with concrete slurry. What a shame, all he wanted to do was farm.

Adapting equipment. (Misuse, in modern terms.)

Ian, me, Eddie and Norman.(I don't know the dog.)
Making a dam . . . or a boat. Adapting equipment to
suit a purpose for which it was not designed.

Our station officer at the time was not necessarily universally popular. I recall one night he had been sent to supervise a rural farm fire and the operational crew heard over the radio that he was mobile to the incident. He had to ask over the radio for renewed directions and if the crew was still at the job. Fire control confirmed the location and that fire crews were still there. To which he replied, 'they seem to be remarkably well hidden.'
They had turned off all lights in the hope he wouldn't find them in the dark.

A quick aside here, about another officer who had parked his car in a field near an incident. As the fire was dealt with and darkness fell, crews were sent back to station. Time for our friend to leave too. Trouble is, it was pitch black and with no torch he had to scour the field for some considerable time before finding his car. Operational firefighters just love a story like that. Which is why I remembered it probably.

**

The Strike

I had joined the Fire Brigades Union while at training school. It seemed a good idea, although the union official was powerless to have my giant trousers replaced – as he had promised.
Prior to the strike in 1977 we had gone on a work to rule for one day. It was most strange, as every normal day we would be either cleaning

something or running around and being suitably shouted at. On this special day, we were only to answer emergency calls and sat around doing very little ... except praying for the bells to go down. And they did ! It was like in the old war films I'd seen with the spitfire pilots running to their machines. The sound of the station bells, the engine revving and the crump of the folding doors opening up onto the street .... music to our ears.

I'd been voted in as branch secretary at Corby fire station (while I was out on a routine fire inspection). I was sort of honoured that they had chosen me but in my heart of hearts knew the job was a poison chalice. Still, I did my best. Once we were out on strike, I had only two days off in ten weeks. There were always jobs to do, social services, collecting wood, picket duty, responding to awkward letters in the newspapers, and trying to raise support from others. I gave a speech to about 400 union members of the AUEW at the civic hall. It was someone else's job, but they called to say they couldn't come .... 'so, get down there and do it yourself!' So, I did.

We were opposed, expectedly by the CBI, unbelievably by the TUC, and inevitably by all political parties apart from the communists, who donated five pounds to our non-existent strike fund.

It surprisingly went well.

Understand this, if nothing else, the good guys were outside on the picket line, many of those who continued to collect their pieces of silver and work though, may have differing views. Rather than lose the good people on strike to other jobs, paying a decent wage would keep the best people employed. Firemen were classed as being in the upper quartile of the semi-skilled manual workers group. Tell that to someone at a chemical spill or when stuck in a crushed vehicle. Let them decide who is skilled. As an example, one fireman had two children and a wife at home. They received benefits, though he did not. More money went into his house as he sat at home doing nothing, than when he was working a forty-eight-hour week, nights and weekends and risking his life. That should give you an idea how poorly we were paid. I rest my case. The police too were losing good long serving officers at the time as well. In general, the police were helpful and understanding, as were most of the general public. Except for one lone and unhappy woman who threatened to burn down our homes.

Beware what you read in the news, the BBC ran different stories to ITV and many newspapers had anti-union axes to grind. There was probably a D notice issued, which prevents certain news from being shared. The truth was out there, but you'd have a hard job finding it. We knew of events that were happening, but they never saw the light of day. The state machinery was not on our side.

The ambulance station next door donated an old settee, and it was placed across the road from the station on a patch of waste ground. Some polythene sheeting was stretched over a wooden frame to keep out the winter rain. As the weeks wore on and the weather became more inclement, we became hardened to spending hours outside on picket duty. After one stormy night, two of our colleagues woke up to find their plastic roof had disappeared and a light covering of snow had decorated their bodies. There is so much I could write about the strike, but time moves on and we had to return and work alongside the blackleg labour that had raked in the money while we had nothing. We just got back on with the job of looking after the public – those who paid our wages and cared for us too. We had to buy back our lost pension debt once we were earning again. An emotive time with scars that may never heal. Making the decision to actually strike was incredibly difficult. A group of men who were dedicated to helping others were forced into a position of removing their labour. Sleepless nights and soul searching was rife. It had to be done though to keep good people in the job. You really don't want a bunch of poorly paid no-hopers coming to your aid. You need dedicated, skilled and caring people. Enough said.

Christmas was different that year, it was in some ways the best we ever had. There was no pressure or expectation from family. My wife and I made some games out of cardboard for our son. He liked them too.

What little was donated on the picket line, be it coins, firewood or vegetables, we shared amicably.

Mick, me and Rod on picket duty
Corby, Northants – the winter of 77

No idea who the dog is, then me on the left.
Photo taken by someone with the shakes.

Those who joined after the 77/78 strike might consider
the benefits enjoyed as a result of our sacrifice.

Corby had its problems, some were like anywhere else, but there was one housing estate where the shop windows and telephone boxes were covered in heavy duty wire mesh. On entering a shop, you were met by an empty counter, behind which stood the shopkeeper and behind him he kept all the shop goods, guarding them from shoplifters. We weren't supposed to go on the estate without a police escort. However, one night we were at a derelict bock of flats, only built a few years before and now stripped of all copper piping and wiring, some flooring and quite a few doors. One of the crew noticed a woman being attacked in the street. He shouted down, 'did you want me to call the police?'

'No,' came the reply, 'it's okay, it's my son-in-law.'

It wasn't unknown for a fireman to have to hang on the back of the appliance as we left an incident to stop kids, who in general sadly saw us as the enemy, jumping on and hitching a ride. I have a feeling that our sub officer alienated the public with his attitude. Some dubious events occurred under his command. Shocking and disappointing events, but he had friends in high places.

It's just one more case of, 'how do they do it?'

**

Silverstone

Occasionally, an opportunity would arise to be a fire marshal at the racetrack. Though it was an all-day job, we were suitably rewarded with one British pound coin, and a plastic wrapping containing a curled-up sandwich and an apple. We turned up in fire kit and they handed us an extinguisher each. Beyond that, no further information was imparted. Safety seemed to be more built on hope than anything else. Much has changed since then. I saw some interesting vehicles racing – only briefly though, as they roared past then disappeared around the rest of the circuit and out of sight. I left with new learning, always worthwhile, and a migraine. Just another experience and a good lesson on why regular visitors wore ear defenders.

**

K433s, it's a number that just came back to me. They were for home office statistics and had to be filled in for all incidents. They included, time of day, road conditions, type of fire, extent of damage, how tackled etc. Well, the system at Corby was collect a few then fill them in at some time before the next week, it didn't matter who did them. In consequence it was rumoured that home office staff would find Corby a highly desirable holiday destination as it was always described as dry and sunny on the forms. Perhaps the sub officer was simply lazy and couldn't be bothered with paperwork after an exhausting stint at a fire.

Corby's water tender.

**

Turnout v attendance fee

For retained firefighters and their wholetime counterparts on a nucleus or day manned station, the first in and who placed their tally on the board would earn a place on the appliance and a few pounds in their bank. The turnout fee was greater than the hourly wage of a wholetime firefighter, so for the first hour at a fire the part timer was more highly paid. Some village stations based near a busy wholetime one could earn small fortunes with calls on standby in the city. Often the 'stop' message would be in before they'd left their village. A good earner indeed for what could easily be a few minutes inconvenience. Those who didn't make the appliance but turned up at station received a lesser, attendance, allowance. If the station had a second pump, then they might still have a chance if the fireground required assistance. Some firemen weren't interested in turn outs and would wait until the appliance had gone, then wander across the road for the lesser fee. For others it was a nail-biting competition to be there first. If your pals saw you responding, then they might open the front doors, otherwise the rule was to enter the station by the rear drill yard – a longer way around. There was one chap that attended by bicycle and lived in the same street as another who attended by car. The chap on the bike, though much slower, would weave from side to side preventing the car overtaking, hence securing a grand victory.

One day, I went for a jog down our street and another fireman thought he'd missed his pager going off and ran to the station. Elsewhere, Paul was so intent for his alerter to activate, that he went in on the sound played in the quiz programme 'Mastermind', and on another occasion on the bleeps at a pelican crossing. He was a keen lad for sure.

**

Changing brigades

After the strike, the station wasn't a pleasant place to work, the officers in charge had been blacklegs and no doubt enjoyed our forced return to work, initially with little to show for it. I could have moved to Northampton but preferred to move eastwards and tried for rural Norfolk and Cambridgeshire. Cumbria too – but I won't share that tale.

Cambridgeshire accepted me and offered a temporary house, which I am convinced beyond words, was definitely haunted. We eventually ended up living way out in the fens. It was a safe place to live, everyone knew everyone else, (often related), the postman would read your postcards before putting them through the letter box and you could leave the keys in your car while going into shops.

We had a large garden, I built sheds, planted trees and vegetables and kept chickens. It should have been a peaceful and happy home. It wasn't to be. Life can be a tad cruel at times, but duty still called and remained my stability.

**

Stanground Fire Station.

This was Peterborough's second whole time station and was located on the south side of the river Nene. The city also had a volunteer station that could man two pumps from their own premises not far from the city centre. There was a fair bit of competition, not always healthy either, between the whole timers and the retained. As I had worked on two nucleus manned stations I was quite used to mixed working arrangements. The volunteers though, had worked during the strike. Such memories die slowly. Stanground wasn't a busy station, about 600 calls a year at the time and about the same as my previous station, Corby. Except at Corby, I could be on nearly every call and here I had to share only a quarter. Sometimes the northern station, at Dogsthorpe, had enough crew on duty to man two pumps. We were hardly ever woken up on nights. I recall one morning, getting up for breakfast and we heard on the news of a four-pump farm fire in a village just outside the city. We couldn't understand why we hadn't been called. Apparently this was a night when Dogsthorpe had two pumps on the run and along with the volunteers, who had to work all night then go to work afterwards, that made four. Control had simply forgotten us. Whatever you think of firemen sleeping on shift, I am confident I can defend it. It worked well – for the people as well as the firemen. I won't bother here, and in any case, they don't anymore.

One snowy day, as the local school children were making their way home past the station, they noticed the caretaker at the window.

Perhaps they knew of his alleged past dodgy reputation, but whatever reason they had, they started to throw snowballs. Some of the watch thought this was fun and joined in. Soon, most of the watch were on the forecourt defending the station from an ever-increasing number of even bigger children from a large school down the road. The watch could see an embarrassing defeat coming their way and retreated into the station appliance bay where they could close the electrically operated doors and be safe. As the doors whirred their way closed, a snowball would break the motion sensor beam, (fitted to stop the doors closing on a vehicle for example), the doors would immediately go into reverse and open again ... too frequently for comfort. The station was filling up with snow by now, as hundreds of kids entered the fray. There was nothing for it but to put a pump into gear and turn a hose reel on the marauding savages to drive them back from breaking the beam. We expected later that day, that lots of angry parents might turn up too, wanting to know why their kids had arrived home soaked.

Blue Watch

53

The station was next to a graveyard on one side and overlooked a field going down to the river on another. There was a man on one watch that liked to pick fresh mushrooms from the field for breakfast. One night, his watch put a white paper plate at the far end of the field. In the morning the victim was ecstatic to see a monster mushroom way down the sloping field and he set off to capture it. As he approached the impending tasty breakfast, the crew put the bells down. (No longer the mind-numbing large bells by then, but a pleasant mellow electronic tone – so as to wake the firemen gently! Reducing heart attacks in later years.) Now, the victim had a heart pounding and embarrassing run all the way back up hill, cheered on enthusiastically by some very amused colleagues.

**

High - Expansion Foam.

Amazing stuff, the foam bubbles could push their way into all manner of spaces, excluding air and smothering the fire. If you walked backwards through it, the bubbles burst and left you with air to breath. As long as it wasn't full of toxic smoke that is.

It was highly disorienting, in that both light and sound were attenuated. The distress signal unit carried on a breathing apparatus set couldn't be heard at all beyond a few feet. One reason that they discontinued sending people into the foam to find and fight the fire. It had its uses. (Mostly at night clubs I might wonder).

**

Promotions

In all honesty, it was only when I believed that the public would be better off with me than with some of those who had risen in the ranks, that I sought promotion. I worked hard and studied, taking my role as a public servant seriously. I never cheated in exams either, unlike so many people I know had done. One of them had a set of firemanship manuals out in the toilets, then there were those with hydraulic formulae written on cigarette papers or scratched into their plastic rulers, one even blatantly had the handbook on fire prevention and legislation on his desk. After gaining a qualification which they were unable to justify, they were promoted and remained in their relative ignorance. Self interest in public servants is not in the public interest.

Sour grapes on my part? Yes you are right.

Once you made leading Fireman you had earned the right (read misfortune) to inherit two of the worst jobs on the station. One, the laundry collection, all the outgoing dirty tea and roller towels had to be counted, stacked and logged and the incoming clean stuff logged and stored. Two, the diesel and petrol fuel tanks on the far side of the yard needed dipping and the amount of fuel logged and correlated with the pump counter. A fairly dirty job that often seemed to coincide with rain. Ah, the rich rewards of promotion.

Later, when I worked at the training centre, we had to assist in the practical exams. One candidate had an acetylene cylinder incident to deal with as his assessment problem. He gathered his entire crew around the cylinder and chatted with them. We instructors were shocked and knew this was an immediate failure. He could have killed them all by ignoring safe practice. He passed! Later he made senior officer level. How could this have happened? Even Masons have principles, don't they? (Allegedly.)

Once I was divorced, I relied heavily upon having a decent meal at work, it was the only proper food of my day. One evening I arrived at work to discover there was no cooking allowed that night and I had a fifteen-hour shift ahead of me, the kitchen had been closed to the watch personnel and handed over to some visiting Germans on a town twinning spree. This upset me greatly, but I could see it didn't bother the officer in charge ... he's the one who made chicken supreme one night and was, as a fire officer, totally useless, he really hadn't a clue. I had had enough. I had been a leading fireman for a good few years but found it difficult to associate myself with such appalling and uncaring management of operational firefighters. I took my rank bars off my shoulder and said, 'you can stick these, I want no part of how this service is managed.' He took them as though being offered a cake and said nothing. I was one of four people on the station that handed in their bars at some point. Didn't that tell them anything at all? Obviously nothing they were concerned about. They let me stay with the watch though, and realising my mistake, I tried many times for promotion. I didn't even make it to the list. Then, one day, I was approached and asked if I was the sort of bloke who could be pushed around. I didn't think I was and said so. A job had arisen on another watch, and I took it. The crews were much the same, the work was the same, it was okay. Then I had a chance of temporary work at the training centre. It was a job that suited me, and I loved it. I had a chance to help others become better firefighters and in turn to keep them safer and yet make a difference to the people we served. When a station officer's post there finally became vacant, they brought in lots of people to try out, none knew as much or cared as much as I did. If they had been promoted I would have had to teach them the job. That would not have been fair at all in my mind. But then, what place rates fairness in this world?

I eventually made station officer and it was a great achievement for me. I tried to live up to the best of ideals.

Shortly afterwards, I went from a forty-two-hour week, day job, to the flexi duty system. A seventy-six-hour week with twenty per cent pay increase. I had to buy an approved, decent car with which to attend emergency calls. There's a whole book's worth just on those experiences. The long weekend was the worst, it consisted of Friday, Saturday and Sunday twenty-four hours a day at work or on call. We'll leave it there.

Except to say, I was once, as a leading fireman, called to the divisional commander's office and asked where my loyalties lay. I pointed to the window and replied, 'to the people out there, who pay my wages.'

'Wrong answer,' I was told. 'The chief fire officer is where your loyalty ends.'

I thought about this, and still do. What if the chief is useless, corrupt, or evil?

There was an earlier time, life was not so good, I had nowhere to live of my own, but a vacancy arose at a station where houses were supplied (and eventually sold to the occupant at a bargain price as it happens). I applied, it was perfect for me, a job I could embrace and do well, and importantly, somewhere to live. The interview went well, so well that the divisional commander had me in his office the next day to commend me for it and tell me that he wished he'd said the things I had. The man who was actually given the job was invited to the same office for a telling off for his own appalling display at the interview. Does this tell us something?

I did the brigade more favours than they ever gave
me. By a country mile.

**

Promotion exams . . . mmm!

The practical exam for sub officer did not go well.
Either the watch was trying to help me by making
some obvious mistakes for me to correct, or they
were determined I should fail by making so many
I couldn't keep up with them. In fact, they made so
many mistakes in securing the suction hose to
work from open water that it must have taken a
genius to organise it. How can you do such a
simple thing so wrong? In the end I gathered the
crews around the light portable pump and
explained the errors. Naturally I failed. Why? No
idea. Why did the watch behave like that? No idea,
but no grudges, just curiosity. A lot of practise goes
into preparing for the tests and the opportunity to
try again wouldn't come until the following year.
Lots of learning required for the standard verbal
instructions, and being able to shout them,
sometimes while running about and pointing. Try
it some time. Shouting is a fire service speciality. I
knew a chap that used his children's teddy bears to
practise the drills, lining them up and numbering
them off. Cries of, 'three paces to the rear of and
facing the appliance, crew fall in. Rest. Still. Stand
from under. The latter instruction to be given if
lowering an object from above or accidentally
dropping something. Never look up when you
hear that one . . . or risk a face full of piano or some
other debris.

60

Section 11d of the Fire Services Act 1947 gave us privileged access to all manner of premises. For all major risks, we carried a folder containing maps, plans and information useful in the event of fire. We were entitled by statutory right at any reasonable time to inspect these places and were issued with identity cards. Inside Cathedral roof spaces, flour mills, research facilities, nuclear bunkers, institutions for the criminally insane, engineering plants, hotels, factories, you name it, we went there. Seeing behind the scenes and looking with critical eyes as to the risks posed in fire or accident was at times a shocking revelation. Sometimes what we knew was secret and we were bound by that. I visited a quite famous potato processing plant once. The scene could have graced any science fiction adventure film, depicting a hell in which people were forced to work and never escape. An almost lightless structure where the firefighter first met toxic chemical baths, then moving machinery and on to vats of boiling oil, then a freezing plant and storage room.

Around us, broken electrical switches, gas cylinders, oil or ice on the floors and all the time in semi darkness. If the power went off during a fire, then likely, nothing closer to hell would be found on earth. (I haven't told you this of course. I still buy their hash browns.)

To be shown what we were, was indeed a privilege, for which I still remain grateful.

**

61

London Salvage Corps

No longer in existence, it was an organisation set up by insurance companies so that in the event of a fire, a team of experts in salvage could be on the scene alongside the fire crews. They could cover over goods with tarpaulins, sheet up roofs and remove flood water etc. The smaller insurance companies began to withdraw their support, leaving the major players to foot the considerable bill of maintaining a fully manned 24/7 service. There came a point where even the big boys thought, 'mmm, this isn't working for us. We are out too.' Or language more fitting that I can't write here.

The organisation was still active when I went on a three-day course in London. During my short stay with them, we had few calls and none that required action. Although we did attend the Old Bailey with some fire crews and took the opportunity to have a look around. As it was the middle of the night the place was empty. A beautiful building though, of ornate and decorated interior. I don't recall doing much while there, in fact I can't remember anything.

**

Smokers and chip pans

Not so much of a problem nowadays but they both presented real life risks in the seventies. A bit of skill is required tackling chip pan fires, if someone foolishly introduces water, even a little, then that turns to steam and expands 1700 times, with devastating results. It wasn't uncommon for drunks to put the chip pan on when they finally staggered home and fancied a snack. Not a good combination. A crew at Corby went to such a fire and the occupant was so inebriated he tried to push his way past the firemen in breathing apparatus so he could go to bed. Not a bad idea to let them put the fire out first, eh? One enterprising soul did the right thing and placed a dustbin lid over the burning oil pan. It would have worked too if it hadn't been made of rubber. It wasn't a severe fire, but his entire house was full of sooty smuts, and he had only just replaced all his doors with swinging ranch style types. Looked nice, didn't stop smoke though.

Smokers? They probably killed a few of themselves off, if not slowly, by fire. We went to a small fire in a ground floor flat on a rough estate in Peterborough. The occupant was obviously an enthusiastic smoker and a rather careless one at that. His settee and surrounding carpet were pock marked with innumerable burn holes. My guess is that he wasn't popular in the neighbourhood as some passers-by shouted, 'let the *^**^^! burn!' Life is not a bed of roses for some. Smokers were a nuisance, they actively started many fires, by choice. That's what a cigarette is after all.

**

Hydrants and water supplies

A wonderful design, bright yellow and easily visible, the top number indicating the size of the main and the lower number how many feet away from the sign. (Yes, they changed to metric later.) So, when snow was on the ground and covering the hydrant pit, all we had to do was stand with our back to the plate and step out the requisite distance. Then they had a cheaper idea. No need for concrete posts, we can hang a hydrant plate on any old street furniture, regardless of angle and distance. So, they did. At the same time, they decided firefighters were underutilised by checking the location and state of a hydrant themselves (though, at the same time learning local risks, topography and interacting with the public), so they stopped them, and employed a man in a van. At another time, in order to save money on diesel, management decided that fire crews were better employed at their stations and not driving about the town, where they might learn from each other, become familiar with street names and water supplies and present an accessible image to the public. To me, it shows a very limited idea of what a public emergency service is about.

Firemen would always slap some yellow paint on a kerb stone (neatly of course) to help locate a plate that may have been screwed to a fence for example. We were told to stop the practice. On a dark rainy night when someone's house is on fire and you are running short of water, you don't give a stuff if there is a bit of paint on a kerb stone. So, we ignored the order. Until of course the job was no longer ours.

Some water mains were made from asbestos. Yes, that's right. Asbestos. They were very fragile and to prevent accidents with water hammer, were only opened and closed very slowly. Some hydrant valves opened clockwise and some not. It was vital you knew which ones went which way. Knowledge of water mains was invaluable. You may have two mains close to each other but the smaller one might deliver more water due to it being a pumping main. Knowing that, can make the difference between success and failure.

Once, in Corby, remembering the population often saw us as an enemy, we were out checking hydrants when a young boy came up and asked me if we were doing the drains. I took this as an opportunity to educate and make a new 'friend'. I explained about the hydrant being a big tap that firemen (and the engine was there, and we were all in uniform) could access in the event of a fire, and that we were just making sure it would work if we needed it. He appeared to listen; the light was obviously on. As he walked away, he saw a pal on the other side of the road and shouted, 'Hey, Mikey, these men are fixing the drains!'

What chance did we have eh?

Rarely would we consider doing so, but by law we could avail ourselves of any water source, even fishponds and swimming pools etc.

I recall one day in particular when a crew of four were out on the 'engine', testing hydrants. The chap I joined the service with, Bob, and I, were in the back. The appliances at that time had concertina doors, so you could drive with them open. (No seat belts back then either.) As we came to each hydrant we would leap out with standpipe, key and bar in hand. We were a team and enjoying the speed of our work. We were still conditioned, read institutionalised, from our time at training school where everything was done at the double. Our driver, Eddie, slowed outside a hydrant and Bob was out like a flash ready to work. Eddie changed down a gear and turned left into a side street where he began to accelerate up the hill. From the open doorway I had a great view of Bob left standing on the corner, his horrified expression, and his determined run to catch us up. Like one of the old laurel and Hardy type films, he slowly appeared in the now fast-moving open doorway. Like the cowboys leaping from a horse onto a stagecoach he made his daring leap to safety. I'm not sure how much our officer and driver knew of the event. Perhaps it was planned. I'll never know now.

**

Places of no return

Though likely to be extremely rare, there could exist situations where firefighters that became contaminated might be lost. The same goes for other emergency services. Taking certain types of radioactive material, pesticides or biological risks. (The recent covid 19 outbreak is an indicator of how bad an 'escaped disease' can be.) An exclusion perimeter can be set up, but those inside it may ultimately have to be expendable in the interests of a greater population. The pesticide-soaked farmer can cost us, the ambulance, the medics who attend, the A&E ward, a doctor and nurses. When you step across the line, you might not be coming back.

All manner of experiments occurred in medical research laboratories. We had instructions for some places that on no account in the event of fire, were we to release any of the caged animals. Though not active during the time of our visit, one laboratory was to work on rabies.

Risks require choices. Not all of them pleasant.

Witness the many young men who died shovelling radioactive spilled material at Chernobyl. They were paid to make one short run on the roof to drop over some small object. That's all. They paid it back with their lives. Risks require difficult decisions and sometimes the ultimate sacrifice. As in the military in war.

67

Training courses for industry

We would run training courses on fire extinguishers and fire safety. Sometimes at a company's premises, other times at a local fire station. We had an old film projector, that whirred and clanked the same old films around its spools time after time. I can remember them well, not surprisingly. One was of a high rise building in 1974 Sao Paulo. The fire chased many of the occupants to the roof. By the time they arrived, the updraught from the fire was too much for any helicopter rescue. People jumped to their deaths to avoid the searing heat. Forty people died doing so or trying to reach ladders that were nowhere near long enough for such a building. Some poor chap's head was split open by impact and the film showed it in stark detail as a priest made the sign of the cross over his body. Graphic stuff to make sure people paid at least some attention to our training. We lit small fires of different types in cut down metal drums, then advised the students how to approach the fire and operate the correct extinguisher. Water on an oil fire can turn very nasty. The water, expanding 1,700 times into steam, can throw burning oil some distance and spreads the fire over a greater area. Inside a room such a fireball could be lethal. Badly burned people might wish they had died instead. Sometimes they did commit suicide. Burned hands meant normal life was over. Think about it. Perhaps you already have. At a burns conference I once had the privilege to listen to Simon Weston speaking on the subject and about the depression that accompanied his injuries. An amazing man, he found a way out.

**

Cambridge drill tower, source unknown.
**

The acid test – a lecture

Usually, on every night shift, we would have drills, station maintenance, and a lecture. Some subjects were very dry to say the least. For example, acids, bases and metals, if memory serves me well enough. I had an idea and was allowed to pursue it. I contacted the local college and 'borrowed' some hydrochloric and sulphuric acids and some small porcelain dishes. I already had a nitric acid bottle. Empty mind you, until I put some water in it. The watch were gathered in the lecture room, and I stood behind the desk and sink on the platform. I explained how dangerous acids were and poured a little hydrochloric acid into a dish. With an extreme warning of caution, I invited them to sniff the acid. It is an impossibility; the first whiff of danger shuts down your ability to breathe any further. They were all impressed. Next was a demonstration of what could happen to our own skin if touched by sulphuric acid. A few drops of acid were added to a small bowl containing sugar. The reaction was instant, and the sugar reduced to a charred mess. This too drew murmurs of appreciation. This was no boring lecture; this was stuff they could relate to in their own world.

Next came the nitric acid, which I then explained was the worst of all. More murmurs of anticipation. As I poured from my nitric acid bottle into a dish, held over the sink, I made a 'sssssttt' noise which I hoped would grab their attention. As I stepped off the platform holding the dish of liquid carefully, reverently even, I created a trip and threw the contents all over the groin area of one convenient fireman. Andy was a larger-than-life figure, always curious, which is why he was actually standing to watch. He struck his normal pose of 'hands in pockets' and was the perfect target. As soon as the 'nitric acid' struck his groin he couldn't get his hands out of his pockets quick enough, and they became temporarily stuck. He jumped about a bit trying to defend his precious private bits. Did the watch leap up in horror? Did they immediately render emergency first aid? No, this band of firefighting brothers just fell about laughing. They were impressed again. Yet only I had known it was water, they didn't!

**

Brigade orders

I suppose because I could spell and had a critically observant nature and a suspicion about how some things were expressed, I ended up writing brigade orders. I did my best to provide readable and useful guidance for my colleagues. I tried to remove the ambiguity of some of the home office edicts (technical bulletins). A case in point was the one on silos. Silos used for storing chemicals or more predominantly animal feed in particular. I telephoned the home office and spoke to one of the fire service inspectors. 'The order on silos. It says that no one should enter a silo to affect a rescue while there is the danger of adhering material above. And that it should be cleared before entry. That means clearing the caked adhering material and it then falling onto the casualty, probably ending a rescue attempt and starting a body recovery.'

'Yes, that's correct,' he said.

It was a relief to speak with someone who was honest about the problem and not waffling ambiguously. The problem... and the solution ... was that an emergency service employer has a statutory duty for their employees and must protect them. They have no such duty to someone foolish enough to enter a dangerous silo and become incapacitated, overcome with fumes or trapped or whatever.

How do we overcome such a dichotomy? We know that if fire control mobilises a crew to rescue someone from a silo, that's what they will try and do. They haven't turned up just to be witnesses to a needless death. They will risk themselves for others. Writing the order needed to explain the truth but allow reasonable steps to be taken while protecting the crew with written backing supported by the brigade. Oh, what a difficult path to tread.

Trench collapse was another interesting order to write, and I did a three-day course at a specialist centre to gain background. I think in the end, legislation came in to make the diggers of the trench responsible for providing rescue.

Breathing apparatus was the big one. For one part of it, to do with emergency crews, it needed a policy decision. Only made by a chap at HQ. I waited six months, and despite having given him a detailed no brainer risk assessment he ended up denying it was ever sent. Finally, we had an answer from him, and the brigade could have their new orders. When you read in my book about the monkey officer, this was him at work ... or not work!

An aside – I noticed that a neighbouring county were using new sets with different cylinder configurations. They had less air than ours but lasted longer. I thought, 'that can't be right, surely.' I phoned the manufacture, who said it was something to do with the laws of physics and pressure laws changed at some point. That just didn't seem right, I mean $p1\ v1 = p2\ v2$, doesn't it? I contacted the neighbouring county as it was important to know whose sets could be allowed for emergency teams if we worked together at an incident.

I explained my query to someone, who went away and came back with an answer, 'my station officer said, mind your own business, we have already issued our orders and we are right, now clear off.' It turned out that they weren't right, they had taken data from the wrong manufacturer's information sheet. The air in their cylinders would not last the time they thought. No apology nor thanks came my way. But then, I was only doing what I was paid for, what more should I expect.

I had to plan my own workload at that time and reasoned that with luck and a great deal of effort I might manage five orders a year. So, I marked my plans on a chart. Operating a traffic light system to indicate the stage I was at. Obviously they were all red at the beginning. In order to stop orders being rewritten the following year, I instigated a system whereby all interested parties, policy makers, trade unions etc could read and amend if reasonable, any draft. They signed that they agreed with the content and file was kept, stating the reasons for any decisions. I thought that it might save someone in the future a lot of work, wasted work. I didn't meet my target, I only managed four. Sadly, that meant an interview with my boss as I was now counted as having failed . . . and must do better. I realised then, that had I said, 'I can do three but actually managed four.' I would have been hailed a hero and probably nominated for the George cross. A funny world isn't it?

I instigated aide memoirs on dealing with various subjects, to be carried by all front-line appliances and officers. Damn good they were and often used at watch level for training. Again, a colour coded system with key points indicated in the correct order of action. I produced a boat training manual as well, foolishly in my own time at home. I combined elements from the Manual of Firemanship, fireboats and ship fires, with various publications on boating and survival. No computer then, just photocopy a picture, cut out the bit I wanted with scissors, glue it on my own page and after adding text, photocopy again. It worked. But I enjoyed the creation of something useful. While in the operation support unit, writing orders, don't think it wasn't the only thing I did. Operational calls and spending time with an allocated retained station were also part of the job.

To be honest, I really needed help by then. I could have achieved so much more if I had an assistant who would relieve me of some less important matters. No help was forthcoming. Not until I met the brigade's psychiatric adviser. (Who they often ignored mind you.)

**

Fire control
(We couldn't have gone anywhere without them!)

When the south Cambridgeshire fire control was based at Cambridge station, from the call coming in, we could be on the road and mobile to an incident in forty seconds. That's not bad by anyone's standards. The reason being, that we would go to the appliance room when we heard the nines bell ring. We knew an emergency call was coming into control, and with about 3,000 calls a year for our station, it was likely for us. Control soon let us know, sometimes with a gesture through the window. Teamwork and efficiency, a real blessing. It all changed when they centralised control, after that, the bells would go down, but we could only turn out after a message was remotely typed into the tele printer, for which we would wait while it click-clacked its slow progress across the page. Development I'm afraid. The close connection between operational firefighters and control staff was broken forever. Shame, so much mutually learned. I miss those people. Always will.

**

The cooks' rota.
At Cambridge, a cook was only available weekdays for tea break and lunch times. Evenings and weekends we had to cater for ourselves. Each watch would have its own mess club and some food items were available from the kitchen store, which was run centrally. Sometimes a crew would be sent out for some essential shopping. If you wanted to eat with the watch, normally sixteen strong on duty, then you were either a cook or a washer up. To be on the cooks list you at least needed to be able to make one decent meal. Some specialised in a curry or spaghetti Bolognese. The cook would also do fried breakfasts in the morning. As I write this, so many hilarious stories come to mind, they would fill a book in their own right. Spaghetti was tested by throwing it at the kitchen wall, if it stuck, then it was ready. Andy cooked curries, the disadvantage in being his

washer up was that he used every pan and utensil in the kitchen. I was pleased when I graduated to cook ... I can hardly remember what I did, but it played havoc with their innards I was told later. Once, Andy, good bloke, made us boiled eggs for breakfast, nicely laid out with buttered soldiers. Trouble is, he hadn't cooked them long enough and they were mostly raw. He wasn't popular. Next day he boiled more eggs, but to be on the safe side he gave them a much longer boiling. They were like rubber. That was the fun of it I suppose. On one fry up, a learner cook decided to spice up the baked beans with chopped raw onion. I have no idea where he got that notion from, perhaps someone wound him up to do it. They were revolting and naturally he was duly and appropriately informed of the matter.

One night our serving station officer said he would make the watch a meal. Chicken supreme, he said he would do. True to his word he brought in a small saucepan in the bottom of which was his 'chicken supreme'. First, there was not enough for one helping let alone sixteen. Second, it had been over cooked, so the fibres had separated. The contents looked like a grey matted lump of an old cat's furball. I think the expression, 'promoted beyond ability' is the kindest way to put it. How some were not sacked due to their actions, amazes me. (Not about cooking, obviously, though we did go hungry that night. It is vitally important to care for the workforce. It really is essential !)

The reluctant washer up - The more you rushed to the big sink to wash the plates, the more likely it was that someone would push you out of the way and take over. The sink faced the window. Behind the washer up was a big central island with the cookers, fat frier and stainless-steel work surface. Dirty plates would come into the kitchen anti clockwise, be washed, carried around to the steamer racks and be sterilised before restacking. There was one chap, who I only ever saw at the sink once in many years, and this was the night. Plates would be dropped into the soapy water for him to wash, he did so and removed the plate to his left for the trip around the kitchen to the steriliser. But they didn't go there, they re-joined the circuit to the sink and were dropped in again and again. He must have washed all sixteen plates about three times each. It was best never to upset people too much. He once complained his dinner was too hot. Next day they took his out of the freezer. Wicked people eh?

**

The Christmas chicken saga

Our watch's day duty fell upon a Christmas day. John had bought two fresh chickens from a market stall and put them in the station freezer with a request for the preceding day watch to leave them out to defrost during the night. Well, duly done, the birds duly defrosted, but the after-death process of decay had continued in the warm kitchen during the night. On inspection they smelled a bit odd, and the green colour was a touch off putting. But are we men or mice? What can possibly go wrong, we'll eat them. This general consensus was later overruled by the cooks, who thought better of it, and the birds were binned. Now we have no meat for dinner. We were joined by a radio reporter who was visiting people who had to work on Christmas day. A good bloke, we called Crocker, told him of our dilemma. He did all the puns live on radio. 'It's something of a fowl problem, though some might say it's a poultry matter, our chicken's gone off and the firemen haven't got a Christmas dinner anymore.'

It wasn't long before the nine's bells were ringing in fire control. They had twenty offers of chickens and turkeys from the general public, swamping the 999 system. A message was quickly broadcast over the local radio not to use the nines and that the problem of a chickenless dinner had been resolved. We took a very kind offer from a nearby terraced street. A driver and I could be spared from the watch strength, and we took a control room girl and her off duty boyfriend with us in a reserve water tender from brigade workshops. While we waited in their living room, our hosts kindly microwaved the huge bird into a defrosted state. It was a kind offer and a truly wonderful Christmas experience.

There's a lot more could be said about Christmas dinners, but it's better left unsaid. Though tempting.

**

*Roof fire in sleet storm, corrugated iron roof cladding
electrified by overhead power line.*

**

*Never esteem anything as of advantage to you that will
make you break your word
or lose your self-respect.*

**

You may travel far but experience nothing.

**

81

At one time, Cambridge fire station had six bays and six appliances on the run. Watch strength was over twenty. Then some bits were scrapped, others moved. More progress.

Nicknamed the 'bread van'
Note – still using wooden ladders.

This smaller than normal, petrol fuelled appliance
was once used as a makeshift rescue vehicle while

the genuine article was in for repair. It was manned with a crew of two and affectionately known as the 'bread van'. One evening we had a call to an outlying village, Steve was driving, and a good driver he was too. As we entered a sharp but seemingly time-altering right-hand bend, I couldn't help feeling we were travelling a little too fast. Possibly within an ace of turning over. I said to Steve, 'that was close.' He replied with typical stoicism, that he had thought so too, and had considered if he might have had to put it into the field. I'm glad he'd kept his plan to himself.

Which reminds me of a few other similar occasions, but I'll stick with just one more. Council workers were all on strike at the time and it was the especially cold and freezing winter of 1978/79. None of the roads were being salted and cleared. The road was a sheet of ice and not surprisingly we were called to a road traffic accident (that's what they called them back then) not more than a mile or two from base. As our driver hurtled on blue lights and two-tones towards the scene, our sub officer (in charge of the crew) spoke, loud enough to be overheard by us in the back, to the driver. 'If you have to put it in the field, do it.'
The lights of the police car and ambulance arrived quicker than expected, well, quicker than our driver expected anyway. Ten tons of lorry would obliterate anything unlucky enough to be in its path. In front, we saw people looking our way in disbelief, one might say utter time stopping shock.

84

Our driver was braking but to no avail, the brakes were on alright, but we had simply become a big red sled on ice. There was just enough room on our side of the road, and we observed astonished faces out of our side windows as we slid by at about thirty to forty miles per hour. Our driver slowly gained control, went to the next road junction, and turned around to drive much more gingerly and appropriately back to the scene. How lucky for all concerned. And concerned they certainly were.

**

The quiz team

Our watch started a quiz team to compete in the national championships. I'm not too sure about the motives of some of our team. 'Shall I wash the appliance room floor .. or ... sit in the warm quiet room and answer questions?' But it didn't matter, we were a team, and we gave it our best. First we knocked out the previous national champions, then neighbouring county teams. There was a zone final at our home station, and one of the opposing teams was one we had beaten before. We were very confident. We gathered around the trophy table and looked at the three trophies, wondering which one was ours. Of the four teams being put to the test that day, we came last, and no trophy. That's life, get over it and pretend it didn't matter!

**

Various collisions of note

Unfortunately, there were lots of them. Too many. I completely redesigned the back end of a Vauxhall Nova, after the driver decided to stop at some red lights and I couldn't. We were in a Chevrolet rescue vehicle, designed for US roads and with a five litre plus engine. Even though the suspension had been altered for our use, it still wallowed at speed. The brakes were either on or off with no finesse in between. They locked up and the front of our vehicle kissed the back end of the one in front . . . enthusiastically heavily. We were mobile to an accident in Hertfordshire where their own rescue vehicle was unable to proceed due to an accident. Hence the urgency. We always said that this vehicle would kill someone one day. We thought it would be one of us. It wasn't. The only damage to the RV (rescue vehicle) was a cracked number plate which workshops fixed easily. We filled in all the necessary accident reports and waited for some sort of inquest or punishment. Oddly, nothing was ever said ! Murphy's law, moments after our prang, the message came through that we weren't required after all.

Having brigade workshops on site was a god send. One night we were mobile to an incident and took a wrong turn, which meant a quick reverse around a street corner. Regardless of my shout and banging the side lockers as hard as I could, the driver managed to reverse into a keep left bollard. It damaged our rear lights and extensively altered the shape of the road furniture. No time to lose we continued to the fire. Afterwards we returned to the scene of the crime, picked up our bits of reflector and in the morning before the day watch came on duty had a word with the mechanics who had it fixed almost as quickly as we'd broken it.

One night, I ventured into the appliance room to find a crew furtively polishing the side of their appliance with metal polish. A well-known trick for hiding scratches that they had accumulated somewhere they obviously wished kept secret. We'll never know.

Not all accidents were reported. As we eased by a yellow Morris marina at some red lights we were preparing to cross, I saw the car tilt away from the appliance. 'Mmm,' I thought, 'that was clever . . . or have we hit it?' On arrival at our incident, we checked the heavy steel bumper. It was mostly black but with a large smudge of what suspiciously looked like yellow paint. We filled in the accident report back at station, but nothing ever came of it. Was the car insured, or taxed, did the driver have a licence? All we did know was his car most certainly had a long dent down the offside.

**

Maskell's bakery and the fireman's tooth.
(True story)

Ah, Maskell's Bakery; I never went there, but ate plenty of their case-hardened bread and rolls over my many years serving at the Fire Station.

Traditional, and bordering on compulsory, cheese and onion rolls or sandwiches were provided for every morning tea break at ten thirty, unless we were out at a fire.

Nice, tasty cheddar cheese, sometimes grated sometimes not, depending on the effort put in by the cook or kitchen duty fireman that had prepared it, and the raw onion, sliced and soaking in a big bowl of vinegar was at the serving hatch for the firemen to help themselves. The best bits were the whole circles in the middle, the coarser large straggly bits from the edges being the last survivors in the bowl.

Now, a bit more about this rare bread; it came in huge industrial scale length loaves with an almost impenetrable crust, except by a big electric powered 'slice everything' machine in the kitchen; you could hear the razor-sharp blade struggling to break through, then suddenly the bakery's first line of defence would be breached, and sharp pieces of crust would flake off and fly like knapped flints, and the blade would continue on its screeching journey.

No exaggeration about those crusts you know. One of the chaps used to cut the crusts off of his sandwiches, much to the amusement of the rest of the Watch, especially as he was an ex 'para', (a past experienced member of the elite fighting unit the Parachute Regiment). One man, laughingly asked the crust remover, nickname 'Rocky', if he would like him, an ex-Royal Marine, to … 'gum his crusts about a bit to soften them up!' This too brought more laughter to White Watch, as they prepared for the 'crust ordeal' themselves. Sometimes a bite of crust could be followed secretly, (you dared not let anyone know you couldn't manage the crusts either), by a swig of hot tea which you would keep in the mouth, pretending you'd swallowed it, until it had begun to soak into the surface of those cursed crusts.

You should have some idea by now about this special, (special awful), bread which we had delivered every day from Maskell's. Did they have some vendetta against us? Had we once let their bakery burn down .... or even a worse fate, actually stopped it from burning down? Or did they use us to get rid of stale stuff that the pig swill man refused to take in the interests of his pig's health?

Now to the man in question. No, not ex-military this time, in fact an ex-milkman from London, where the worst thing in his experience was on delivering to the very top of a high tower block, the customer would say, 'extra pot of yoghurt today, please!' He was big built and powerful, in a relaxed sort of manner, and he was an intelligent man – in a strange academic sort of way, but not in any practical way – he came from a good family in a posh part of London and now lived in any old bed-sit he could find.

He was rich and he was poor.
On pay day he was rich and lived like a King – for about two days – and then he was poor, living off credit from the mess club and everywhere else for a further twenty-eight days.

It was a continuing cycle for him, and us.

Now to the incident itself. It was otherwise an uneventful morning after ladder and pump drills in the yard earlier, when we all gathered around the long mess hall tables with our big white mugs of tea and our precious cheese and onion snacks; I recall I was sitting opposite Paul when he suddenly stopped chewing and an extremely thoughtful expression tumbled down his face. It had happened.

'I've broken a tooth!' he said, horrified. Then, after a good rummage through the half-chewed contents of his mouth, even more horrified, 'It's gone ... not there .... I must've swallowed it ...!'

Anyone would have thought he'd designed this as a comedy sketch to amuse the Watch at tea break, as loud guffaws of laughter broke out and filled the mess hall.

(To you, dear reader, this might seem unkindly, to laugh at such as this, but it was ever so in the ranks of firemen that they would find great merriment in the mishaps and downfalls of each other, ... no one was safe .... but then, no one was hurt. It's what they did.)

Well, Paul went to the dentist, who was obviously a psychic or certainly a good judge of a man's wealth, because he made Paul pay up front for the treatment. Thirty quid it was .... a lot of money in those days, probably only God knows where the money came from, I'm sure Paul didn't!

Eventually Paul was fitted with a small plate to which was attached his fine new tooth. It

90

looked ok, but it was destined to have a flaw … it was a little loose, that's all!

This was to cause a few problems for the tooth's new owner, for example, we would sometimes use, for breathing apparatus (BA) training, some concrete ventilation tunnels that ran under a city centre shopping complex. The tunnels were long, had twists and tight corners, lightless, had occasional changes of level by raking ladders and at times were so low that crews were forced into the, all fours position … and still dragging out their 'rescued' dummy person.

During such an exercise I was the entry control officer and Paul was one of the BA wearers. I could hear the sound of dragging bodies, scuffling gloves and knees and the loud sound created by compressed gas breathing getting nearer, then out came Paul easing his bulk through a small grill opening and dropping a short way down onto the concrete service road where we had set up. He removed the full-face mask to reveal one hot, red and sweaty fireman. He then, without a second to waste, started to search the interior of the face mask, recovered his tooth and replaced it in his mouth along with its fellows. Apparently it had come out quite early in the exercise and had been roaming wild and free in the dark and saliva filled wastelands of the inner mask, … there was nothing Paul could do about it until he completed the job and could remove the mask on the 'outside'.

This looked like it would become a continuing saga, but surprisingly the problem was soon resolved, in a most unusual manner.

One day Paul was out, being driven by one of his girlfriends, when an uncaring City driver drove wildly close causing her to swerve; Paul was inclined a little in the way of a 'judge, jury, and executioner' type man, and opened the window and hurled what I can only guess would be some violent obscenities after the driver. Sadly, what was also hurled out of the window was his new plate and tooth, which being loose had shot out of his mouth and on to some unsuspecting bit of tarmac.

By the time they had stopped, turned around and driven back to the vicinity of the escapologist tooth, it was nowhere to be found. It had achieved what it had strived for ever since the dentist fitted it – freedom. It was lost forever. Paul returned to the dentist and I'm sure you have guessed – the dentist made him pay again – up front!

Maskell's special armoured five pence bread rolls had a lot to answer for.

**

A messy job this one – a council paint store.
Well, it was before the fire.
Note the ladder top right. Pitched on the slope as it
was, it made for some interesting thoughts for those of
us who had used it.

**

Some silly things from some quite brave men.
(Some pranks, mistakes and odd incidents.)
Fire service humour takes the sting out of tragedies
without dishonouring the victims. It is an
invaluable tool to retain sanity in the twisted world
of disasters and heartbreak.
Most, if not all these events are now illegal and
could result in cases of harassment, with the

victims receiving huge compensation. Back then it was simply good fun.

But today I'd like to remember a good fire officer colleague who has not been with us for many a year now.

We all had fire kit; Boots, Helmet, Tunic and over trousers ... oh and leather gloves too. We worked in the fire/smoke house where temperatures would often be over 100 degrees Centigrade. In consequence our gloves would be soaked in sweat. Now that's not such a bad thing if the sweat is yours, but John had the habit of borrowing other people's gloves, it didn't matter whose, any would do.

Nothing much seemed worse to us when we were next to enter the fire building for an exercise and discover cold damp gloves on our hands ... soaked in John's sweat. You cannot deny he was a hard worker, diligent, long serving, honest and reliable. You could also rely on him to have used your gloves !

What some of the other officers did was find an old pair of gloves and join them together with a long piece of string, then thread the string through the sleeves of John's tunic. So, when he went to pick up his tunic, a pair of gloves hung from his sleeves . . . just like a mother does for a very young child. It was a good day, the day of gloves in sleeves.

Young lady walking by.

Many of the fire station doors I've known were solid wood up to about chest height, depending of course on how tall you are, then beyond that, glazed panels up to full height. Occasionally a fireman 'just' on his way from starting or finishing a job might stop to peer into the outside world for a moment. . . or longer if not caught. On occasions it might be better to be caught by an officer than your own work colleagues, your 'good friends'. I recall seeing one such unfortunate who just happened to be staring out of the windows as a charming young lady walked by. Such a coincidence, eh? Trapped and pressed hard by about five strong men keeping low against the doors, his face nearly touching the glass he was powerless neither to escape nor to stop someone banging on the glass next to him. The young lady turned to see what was up. Any expressions of innocence on our fireman's face were easily misconstrued as a hand knocked on the glass repeatedly. The young lady walked off disgusted, the victim sank into embarrassment and the rest of them fell about with laughter. Happy days.

The Squirrel. (Another prosecution coming up !)

The squirrel was dead, long dead before it was found in a nearby park by visiting fire crews. It was driven back to the station where it was going to spend many days entertaining various groups of firemen, (watches). At one time, our grey squirrel, which I have to say looked in rather splendid condition considering it was so long dead, was hidden in a man's locker so as he opened the door it would swing out face height on a piece of cotton. It also adorned the outside of someone else's locker door for a few days. It vanished for a while and we wondered where it had gone, never knowing where it would turn up next. Then one day it was found in the kitchen fridge, probably for the cook's benefit. . . they said they had washed and dried it first!

Tea breaks were a favourite time for the fire crews, a mug of tea or coffee, (tea was made at least half an hour before drinking and consisted of one tea bag for each person plus a handful for the pot. . . you could creosote a fence with it) and a cheese roll or sandwich. . . lovely. A member of the watch offered to fetch the sub officer's sandwich and tea, and as he sat looking out of the upstairs mess room window his plate was set before him. It was a sandwich of two whole slices of white bread and sticking out of one side was a squirrel's bushy tail! I don't think he ate it. After that the squirrel disappeared, who knows where to. It probably gave more amusement in death than it ever could have in its life. Of course, these days the kitchen would be closed down by environmental health, awaiting a judicial review, the men prosecuted by the RSPCA or league for the protection of rodents and probably a few sacked for harassment with a deadly weapon. . . I mean dead weapon. Ah, happy days.

The makeshift spider.

One enterprising watch decided to 'manufacture' a large spider. They attached it to some fishing line and controlled it from a top floor room of the fire station. At night, the 'spider' was lowered from a large tree between the station and the pavement below. They had great fun watching the various responses of the public to this unnaturally huge beast. There were people who took a 'double take', not sure if they were actually seeing something or if it was illusion, then there were those who shuddered and walked on quickly, never looking back. It was highly entertaining.

Unbeknown to them one of their colleagues donned an old coat and a cloth cap, borrowed a bicycle from the station cycle shed and went around the back street to approach the station and tree on his left. They watched this 'doddery' cyclist approaching and saw the perfect victim. With practised skill they lowered the 'beast' to perfection. . . the old guy on the bike was startled. . . hilarious. The old guy wobbled on his bike. . . even more funny. The old guy fell of his bike and lay 'lifeless' on the ground. . . suddenly not so funny. Heart attack? Had they killed him? What should they do? The spider was retrieved, and the evidence tidied away. A couple of the more conscientious hurried downstairs and out into the street lit drama, they were only a short distance from the Police station, it wouldn't be long before the 'body' was discovered. Not sure what state they would find the old gentleman in, but fearing the worst, they gently turned him over to be met by the smiling face of their own watch member. I don't think the spider had any more outings. . . I think it went on a very long holiday!

The mad marine and his nose trick.

It was an important day, the whole watch, about eighteen or so of us, along with a gaggle (best word for them) of officers were to visit a large electricity substation so that we could learn about them in the event of fire or accident. One of the strange things we did discover was that a stray cat had once entered one of these places and shorted out a good size portion of the city. . . and it lived to tell the tale; Eight lives left. Here too is a tale of 'life or death'.

JD as I'll call him, was an ex-marine and a great fire-fighter; he was also given to strange behaviours that could unsettle other watch members, for example he could patiently wait inside someone's clothing locker for their return. It was always a shock when he leapt out and 'got' them. We took to warning each other if we'd seen him on the station. He would also sneak up to a higher floor by climbing the pole in the pole drop, (normally you'd slide down it in response to a fire call); you never expect to meet someone coming the other way!

Where were we? Ah, yes, his nose trick. The material didn't matter, a piece of bread, a piece of paper, anything really, he'd pick it up unseen, then roll it about into a small ball, fiddle with it in the entrance to his nose as though that was where he'd just found it, and then flick it at someone. Yes, I know, horrible eh? Right, back to our visit to the substation; Another chap on our watch was a vegan and was most particular about caring for his diet and his person. Though tragic at the time, it was fortuitous for this story, that at the same time JD was active with his 'nose trick', our vegan colleague was in mid yawn. It couldn't have been a better shot, the rolled-up material went straight into his mouth and hit the back of his throat where it was accidentally swallowed in shock, despite frantic and desperate coughing by the throat's owner. The vegan reaction to this assault on the 'Temple' was aggressively out of character, 'what was it?' he demanded. JD was a bit taken back and explained, 'it was only a bit of leaf', he said.

'What leaf, what plant? Is it poisonous?' came more questions, none of which JD could answer. Well, he didn't die, and nothing will ever dampen the humour of this strange event. JD never changed. . . I bet he still does it to this day.

'Haul Away.'

When I joined the fire service I was stationed at a very quiet little place that was built about 1900. Like most stations it had a drill tower the inside of which doubled as a hose drying tower. (The coating on the inside of early canvas hose was made of rubber and if left wet would form an acid which damaged the hose. . . hence the need to dry it well!) In our drill tower we had a long metal raking ladder to the top where you could stand on a sort of inner balcony. At ground level, hose would be folded in half and the 'bend' hauled aloft by a line (rope) that went over a pulley in the tower roof. A fireman would wait at the top with a strong wooden spar, which would be inserted to hold the hose in place.

My mentor and good friend Eddie one day showed me how you could haul yourself aloft; the line, (calling it a rope was almost a hanging offence), was only a general-purpose type and not designed nor tested for live rescue purposes. None the less, Eddie would tie a bowline knot around his chest and grasping the other free end of the line, haul himself with ease up the tower. It seemed strange that it was so easy to lift yourself like so. I might not have been clever enough to work out the physics of it but was clever enough not to haul myself aloft beyond a recoverable height should the line or pulley fail. A few years later I was standing in a different hose tower in another County; I remembered Eddie's impressive actions and shared the story.

'No, can't be right,' said one.

'Give it a try', encouraged another who had no wish to try it themselves. In the end, one of them grasped the free end of the line and placed his feet in the loops that were used to haul hose aloft. He was a big chap and strong. He pulled on the line, and it moved much easier than he thought, it lifted his feet so easily off the ground... success, we have lift off . . . but this is where his method parted company with Eddie's, once his feet were off the ground there was nothing to keep him vertical, in consequence he rapidly went horizontal. . . now there was no body weight to counteract his pull with his arms, with nothing to hold him up he landed flat on his back, having pulled his own feet from under him. We left the hose tower, some bemused, some laughing, some disappointed and one with a sore back. They lost interest in the story after that. . . . but I haven't!

Before my time at Rushden, they decided to carry out a live recue drill. (In the early days live carry downs were common. It built great trust in your comrades.) Back to the rescue. Phil, a slightly built man, tied a bowline around his chest and was lowered from the inner platform at the top of the drill tower. They learned a lot from this experiment. One, not to repeat it. Two, cutting off the blood supply under the armpits can render one unconscious. Yes, by the time he was lowered to the ground he was sleeping comfortably. Or not, as the case may be.

The village pond

Not far from Cambridge, one of the several pretty villages was experiencing a problem with the local pond. The water level was very low, and people were concerned for the fish and ducks. A call to the fire service resulted in the deployment of a crew and appliance to the rescue. Sure enough, there was little water left in the pond. Setting into a hydrant, it wasn't long before the pond was filled again, leaving happy villagers to celebrate. Well, it wasn't too long after that, some very unhappy people contacted fire control. Yes, the pond had a leak, but in order to mend it, the council had to drain it at some expense in time and money. They weren't happy at all we'd filled it again before the repair was made.

The layby fire
A similar story. It was night-time, and we were alerted to a large fire in a layby between Rushden and Wellingborough. Because of its location, lots of drivers called it in. We arrived at a large heap of entangled tree branches and other material. We put it out with some difficulty. The next night we had a repeat call. Same place, same fire. Eventually it was discovered that workmen trying to burn the rubbish took all day to get the wet wood to light again. When evening came and they went home, we would turn up and put it out.
Communication is a necessity, wouldn't you say?

Help yourself. . . the food wagon.
Not one of my stories this, but never mind. When fire fighters were stuck for prolonged periods at a fire a long way from their station they would be sent out tea and food, usually bacon or cheese sandwiches. It was such an evening and the duty crew on station all mucked in and worked in the kitchen preparing the relief food for some deserving firemen battling a serious fire in appalling weather conditions. They would be tired and hungry by now. There was only one man who

didn't help make the sandwiches, a lazy chap by all accounts, but it had fallen to him to drive the refreshments to the fire ground, using the station van. The first-floor kitchen was linked to the ground floor near the van by a dumb waiter or small goods lift. They gave lazy boy the shout that all was ready, and he reluctantly set off for the fire-ground. Some time and many miles later he arrived, much to the joy of the working crews; they gathered around the back of the van and our lazy boy slowly climbed of the driver's seat, sauntered around to the rear doors, opened them without even looking and said, 'there you go, help yourselves!' The hard-working crews desperate for their refreshments stared into the empty van. There was nothing there, it was all back in the dumb waiter. . . but not as dumb as the bloke that left them there.

Not so funny snacks.

Our training centre had a visit by a group of Royal Marines one day, they were there to experience a little of life as a fire-fighter. To be sure, we wouldn't have been happy to put up with what they had to on their visit. Trouble with a disciplined service is that you must obey orders. . . even if they seem totally stupid. You have to respect the rank of the officer even if the man himself is a complete plonker. . . it is just something you have to put up with. Well, our boss was one of them. The emergency rations held on the mobile incident support unit were just creeping

103

past their use by date. 'What a splendid idea', he must have thought, 'instead of spending good money on these Royal Marines, I'll give them the out-of-date pasties, then claim for a completely new stock of tasty in date ones, my God I'm so clever. Hey, I've just had another brilliant idea,' he must have continued, probably admiring himself in the mirror as he did so, 'we can use the microwave on the operations unit to show them how charitably we care for our brave fire-fighters at prolonged incidents.'

The trouble is he didn't know how long it took to microwave a pastie into the edible range from the frozen state. If you know anything about microwave cookers you'll be well in front of me by now. To defrost and heat one pastie was taking about ten minutes, and even then they were a bit frozen in places, there were about 15 or 20 soldiers, so that's 15 x 10 = 150 minutes or two and a half hours! Meanwhile the duty fire-fighters had a very pleasant, cooked dinner in the station mess room. Funny? Not sure it is really. . . it is more sad than anything.

They'd have enjoyed a decent meal and a chance to banter with the fire crews if I was in charge. It never happened.

The sneeze trick.
(There are so many to tell, or not, as the case may be.)

One of the firemen, Roger, sadly not with us anymore, was a very careful, 'conservative' sort of chap. Even when in uniform he 'appeared' to have on a waistcoat with a fob watch in his pocket, a sort of gentleman farmer manner about him. He was standing close by our little group when one of our number, known as 'Rocky' for turning up to work one day with a black eye, said, 'don't say anything, watch this, just ignore what happens and carry on talking.' Well, we weren't sure what he was on about until he dipped his fingers in his drink and, having observed that Roger was looking away at the time, flicked his wet fingers at him, simultaneously making a sneezing noise. Roger's reaction was instant, his head whipped around like a startled cobra to look at the group, probably expecting an apology. None was forthcoming, and we were doing as asked, just chatting away as though nothing had happened. We guessed the big laugh was still to come. Roger took out his handkerchief and dabbed at the wet spots he could feel over his neck and face, examining the damp patches carefully for any evidence. The expression on his face was a real picture. He glared and he dabbed, and we ignored him . . . that was the funny bit really. In the end we had to tell him, I'm not too sure he believed us and failed to see any humour in the jape at all. We did! I've tried it myself a few times. . . be warned, careful who you do it to!

PS Rocky is not with us anymore either. Sad to see people go.

We may have had our disagreements at times, but the watch would soon close ranks, and as one, would face any outside threat together. Regardless of the danger. There was a pride in being a member of the watch.

Mirrors causing trouble

My mentor, Eddie, once told me of a fire he was attending in a large house. As he fought his way in breathing apparatus through the smoke, he came across another crew, who he suspected was from another station a few miles away. 'Strewth', he said, 'you got here quick.' Then realised he was talking to himself in a mirror.

Some years later in Cambridge, at an alarm for a hotel, as we turned up, the station officer was in front and ran down the stairs. Quickly followed by our sub officer, (good man called Basil). Basil saw the back of the station officer running along a corridor and away from him. He followed, then, 'bang', he hit the mirror at the bottom of the stairs. The corridor had taken a turn, but the reflection made it appear to be straight ahead.

We learn from experiences – and sometimes those of others.

**

The risks were everywhere, where do they end?

My turn at the head of the TTL

This was a research lab fire, within the curtilage of a major hospital.

High voltage equipment, radioactive materials, biohazard, cylinders, chemicals, building construction, (floor burned away). Toxic fumes and smoke.

Unbeknown to us until much later, animals died in there (and so did many years of valuable research too).

I recall an excitable Divisional Officer screaming angrily from the doorway at some firemen, 'Get in there now.' That was moments before he fell through the burned-out floor and took on a sheepish look. Always lessons to learn at fires.

With bomb scares, we were the luckier service, it was a police job to investigate, it was ours to attend once the event had occurred. Before that, our orders were to hide behind something substantial. Always follow orders, eh? Those particular ones more than ever.

Fire, flood or gale, we were out.

We had just returned to station after attending a building collapse, where the brickwork from a gable end was completely lifted out by strong wind and dumped into a busy street. Nothing much we could do with that. The council workers would clear it. Yes, councils back then actually employed workers to undertake physical work. Our next call was to a man trapped under a roof. We made haste to the address and ran to the rear of the property. Some surprised occupants came out and asked what we wanted. When we explained, they pointed us in the direction of their neighbour's house. We knocked and a little old lady answered the door. We enquired about a man reportedly trapped. 'Ah yes,' she said, 'he's up there.' Pointing to the ceiling trap door. It still looked like we could have a real task on our hands. Then she concluded, 'it's Benny from Crossroads.' (A simple bloke with a woolly hat from a rubbish TV soap series.) A policewoman spoke to her, 'We've been here before, haven't we?' It required no answer. We couldn't leave though without checking the roof space. Would you stick your head into a darkened space where 'something or someone' might be lurking? Even only in imagination. Luckily an officer, who we will meet several times in this book, did the deed. We did expect (or was it hope?) to see his headless corpse drop from the ladder. It didn't.

The gale late on the 2nd (into the 3rd) of January in 1976 was one of the most severe to affect the British Isles in the twentieth century. Gusts of over one hundred miles per hour were recorded. I was on duty that night and it wasn't long before the bells went down, and we were called to attend an incident in a nearby town. Much I cannot remember, I do remember who was driving though, it was a big chap of 16 years' service called Norm. We turned out of the fire station in the Water Tender, a pumping appliance that carried a 10-metre ladder. We had a shared radio scheme with the police, who were so busy that night, any chance of contacting our own control was completely out of the question. We could see bright flashes of light piercing the darkness as power cables came down across the county. We had to drive over a humped bridge on route, as we did, the wind momentarily lifted the ten-ton vehicle off the road. Evidenced by the driver's shout about his steering had disappeared. He seemed quite excited about it. They say that some people's garden sheds were blown away, never to be found.

The great October storm

"1987 evening of 15th and morning of 16th October. After a wet period, with trees still in full leaf, a deepening storm moving north-eastwards from the Bay of Biscay towards the central North Sea, produced winds of well over 100 mph across the SE part of England after midnight of the 16th.

Eighteen people died, with considerable damage to property, and the loss of 15 million mature trees. The affected area was roughly southeast of a line

110

from Lyme Bay to Lincolnshire, with the maximum damage across London, Home Counties, East Anglia & Kent."

A colleague and I were out all night in the rescue vehicle, using the chain saw to effect wherever we were sent. As dawn broke we were called back into the city and in the growing light witnessed the devastation. The roads were littered with fallen trees past which we had to carefully weave our way.

No railway trains were running, London stations closed with damaged roofs, and a sinking ship had closed part of Dover harbour. With typical tenacity and lots of help from a good friend, myself and partner made it to Bruges for a weekend holiday. No trees down over there.

Amazing what we can go through and still achieve. When we look back on it, we wonder how it could possibly be done. But it was.

During one of the gales, we received a call to a TV aerial in danger of falling on to a public path. It was located at a busy road junction near the railway station, causing us problems in parking. The building was three storeys and had a long sloping slate roof leading up to a large chimney stack . . . and our offending aerial. If it was falling the other way onto private property we wouldn't be involved. We slipped and pitched our longest ladder to just under the guttering, (had we gone above it, then the guttering may have failed and in any case would not give a suitable grip for the head of our ladder). John, an athletic type and later to become a physical training instructor, climbed to the head, carrying our roof ladder. I have no idea how he managed it with the roof and guttering creating an overhang to negotiate, but he did, he managed to just about reach the ridge with the hook of the roof ladder, but it still left a few slates between guttering and 'safety!' I thought I'd better climb up and make sure he was okay. As I reached the top and peered over the guttering, the ladder moved sideways. Not far, but it was enough of a warning that the wind was too strong for safety . . . mine for a start! I called him back down and told him we would request attendance of the turntable ladder. A bit of overkill for a TV aerial but infinitely safer in the circumstances. John re-joined us on the ground having somehow negotiated the overhang a second time. His skill and courage could never be doubted, nor is he forgotten.

The cold
In February 1991 the temperature over a wide area did not rise above freezing between the 5th and 10th. The lowest temperature reached during the month was minus 16.0 degrees C in north Yorkshire. The 7th was believed to be the coldest February day of the century in some places. On the 8th, the maximum at Princeton, on Dartmoor only rose to minus 6⁰ C.

It wasn't just at work that I found challenges, my private life had plenty of disasters too.

Moving Day. . . Moving on the eighth!

We were parting company, my second marriage was over, and so was living in a 4-bedroom detached house with double garage, huge garden with ponds and one acre paddock with stables. The 'good life' was over.

A new day dawned, and a very different life beckoned from the unknown.

I'd planted many a tree in the garden over the few years we were there and every one of them protected by a rabbit guard. 'Careful,' someone had said, 'Rabbits eat the bark for a starter.' However, I never had trouble with rabbits and neither did I know why. . . not until the day we moved.

We had little money and were selling the house for less than we paid. Due to my wife's sudden unemployment difficulties our income had dropped to a level where even my entire wage was insufficient to pay the mortgage. The building society didn't mind us not paying for a while, as there was a lot of equity in the property, and they could easily recover their money.

So, for us both it was off to pastures new, complete with new mortgages and our own old goods and chattels.

We had no money, but I've told you that already, and as a result I was to do all the removals myself. Armed with a heavy goods vehicle licence, I hired a large (dirty great thing) lorry from a town about thirty miles away at a good price because my sister worked there, and I parked it between ours and the neighbour's house on a shared driveway overnight.

Up early the next day, as the new people were moving in at noon, everywhere was white. A heavy fall of snow had visited us silently in the night, as had a severe frost too. We put on the TV for the news just as the newscaster warned. . . 'All over Britain lorries are stranded as diesel freezes,' she said, 'minus eight degrees is quite common. . . roads are treacherous. . .'

It was the 8th of February 1991.

I was too busy to enjoy the snow and explore the myriad of fox tracks that covered the ground. So that's why there were no rabbits and it also explained why the previous occupants lost all their ducks and chickens. You don't need rabbit guards on trees, all you need is a local den of foxes.

The news reported that 'snow fell extensively and often heavily between the 7th and 9th, leaving a covering exceeding 10 cm over large areas of

England, Wales and eastern and southern Scotland.'

Snow or not, furniture had to be moved. Good job I was strong back then. Did it all alone, moving my wife's furniture to Cambridge then returning to load my own to take in the opposite direction of Huntingdon. There I was met with a surprise. Something had gone wrong with the financial transfers. Everyone was in their new home but me. With frozen feet in old trainers that had been cold and wet since early morning, they finally let me have a key at 15.30 hrs. I stored everything in one room. The place had been unoccupied for three years. There was a gas fire in the living room, so I thought, 'hell, I'll go and turn the meter on and pay the price later.' But there was no meter, it had been removed! All water in the house was frozen. I lay on an old and very thin fire brigade mattress, covered myself with a heap of clothes etc and waited for hypothermia to take me off on the deep sleep. Obviously I survived. It took about a year to make the place into a new home. But that's what we do, we don't give up. (Well, not often.)

**

Horse in a ditch

They say, never hoist a horse up by its feet, you may break its legs or affect its vital organs. But this horse was already upside down and wedged firmly in a ditch. Luckily the rider had fallen clear or would most certainly be dead. I realised at this job that my ability to engage properly in the action was waning. The operational crew that were there were working away with all the enthusiasm and strength that was once mine. We were blessed, and so was the horse, by the presence of a veterinarian that worked for the university of Cambridge at the animal research centre. He was used to tying horse's legs with a special knot and hauling their unconscious bodies from one place to another. The banking of the ditch was smoothed out by enthusiastic digging that created more of a slope than a wall. The horse was winched out over a canvas sheet, released, and stood happily back on its feet, about which it had probably wondered earlier why they were pointing skywards. I had taken a series of photos of the rescue and told the junior officer to send the stop message from himself. After all, he had done the work. I believe in credit where credit is due. The developed photos were later given to the watch to assist learning on the station. Just in case they found another upside-down horse.

**

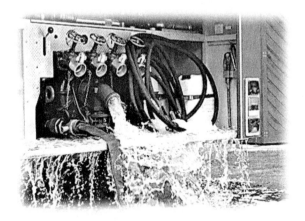

Insurance

Or lack of it. There was a period of time that approximated with the Thatcher years, when all too often, households we attended had no fire insurance. What little they had, was gone. Yes it seems daft and of course it was their choice, but it did seem to be all too frequent an occurrence at that particular time. Bankruptcies and insolvencies were also commonplace. There were those who sought to capitalise on a claim too. Like the family that prior to the unfortunate and of course shockingly accidental fire, moved all their good stuff into a neighbour's house and replaced it with a TV that didn't work and a sofa from the dump etc. Even a scrap car left close to the window – they could only hope, eh? On the same estate, brand new council garden fencing was being taken down to burn on domestic fires. Life can be like that.

**

Radioactive clock and gas mantles

Appliances carried dosimeters, (for measuring exposure to ionizing radiation) the rescue vehicles carried radiation detectors for alpha, beta and gamma. In the cupboard of the sub's office, where the junior officers ran the watch, stood an old alarm clock with the glass removed. It emitted alpha particles from the radium paint, (luminous paint). At the time of manufacture, radiation poisoning was an unknown side effect. Alpha didn't penetrate the glass but once ingested, the particles would do much damage. Whereas gamma rays pass straight through us, and the damage is more transient. The cupboard also held another source, a gas mantle, radioactive thorium. Amazing isn't it, all those old broken mantles crumbled to dust and people would brush it away, even blow on them, not knowing the horrors the dust had in store. When we did our routine checks we would turn on the machines and listen to the ticking counts. Background radiation, that's cosmic rays and the like, ran at about ten counts per second. When the Chernobyl incident occurred, background radiation doubled to twenty counts per second. That is some small indication of just how much material was released over Europe. Nuclear war was and still is a possibility and plans were prepared for the event. Some of them were silly plans . . . and you really don't want to know!

**

Coins, keys and nylon.

If you valued your skin, you wore no nylon clothing, sported no jewellery, and carried no keys or coins. Once in a heated environment, the specific heat capacity of metal means it heats more easily than other materials. In so doing it can reach temperatures able to redden skin. (Burns).

We had an illustrated talk on a specific event, the motor vessel 'Pointsman'. Breathing apparatus wearing crews were sent into the depths of the vessel to fight a fire. Some error of judgement by the captain occurred in the ventilation system being operated with the fire consequently increasing in severity. The crews had to evacuate the ship. The heat was so great that the plastic leggings of the first man on the vertical ladder melted onto the face mask of the BA wearer following. Sounds grim, sounds downright frightening. They showed photographs of the survivors and every reddened skin area was associated with carrying keys or coins or the wearing of metal buckles.

Nylon was also avoided due to its characteristics in fire. Melting point just over 200 deg C and if burned onto skin it can fuse to it, rendering it impossible to separate. Not nice either. God bless cotton and wool eh? Interestingly, some cyanide gas is given off from burning wool. Can't win, can we?

**

Ambulance Chasers

A rare and unusually stupid breed of human that gains pleasure from following emergency vehicles. On this occasion, it followed one of our pumps to a night-time village incident, even going through red lights. This incensed our driver, Roger, and on arrival he walked back to give the driver a piece of his mind.

He even shoved his head inside the car and gave the bloke a jolly good fireman-like telling off (to put it mildly). He also reported the incident to the police.

Later that night, the police contacted the fire station to let us know they had caught the alleged perpetrator but wouldn't pursue a prosecution on the matter as he had been arrested for armed robbery instead. Apparently this excitable gunman that Roger had given what for, had robbed a shop at gunpoint earlier that evening. Who's a lucky chap eh? Made us smile though.

**

Traveller's sites

I went to a few for various reasons and on a personal basis never once had any trouble at them. I never judged the people, I just turned up to do a job. For a short while I was seconded to a liaison panel, consisting of social workers and police. Often the older generation had lost control of the younger ones. I went to a grass fire on one site when we were called in by the residents. 'Grass fire, gas cylinders involved.' Old butane gas cylinders were scattered in a burning field next to their caravans. I arrived first in my car and asked if I could park next to one caravan. The chap in the deck chair was friendly and told me I could. He also told me that the dog next door was the only one on site which was safe to touch. I appreciated his attitude and worked out a plan for when the pump arrived to extinguish the fire from sheltered positions. All went well. No trouble and a cheery wave goodbye from the bloke in his chair. No doubt grateful that no exploding cylinders would spoil his day, or his caravan.

Contractors building the raised bypass hadn't made a good job of it. The banking was slipping and collapsing. The solution was to remove soil, take it somewhere and mix it with lime before returning it to site. They chose a piece of land right next to a traveller's permanent site. One with small brick buildings for accommodation. We had a call from a lady on the site. On arrival we could see the problem, the lime was airborne and choking/burning the people down wind. Holding her small child, she said, 'we are people too.'

And she was right, and the contractors were wrong. There was little we could do to redress this blatant unfairness. Though we did report the matter, I don't know if they listened. Sometimes a deaf ear saves a lot of work. The 'I didn't see it guv,' approach to responsibility avoidance.

**

Fair warning
In the dark, a pond covered in duck weed can look
remarkably like a lawn. It isn't!

**

One eye on the destination means
only one eye on the path.
and
Do not look where you fell,
but where you slipped.

**

Fate and the child in the doorway
The fire was in the garden at the back of the house,
the hose was run out, but we needed water on.
Wearing full fire kit with heavy boots, as I ran
quickly towards the street and the pump operator,
I arrived at the side door of the house just as a small
child stepped out directly in my path. The very
next step would have struck him down, and I have
no doubt seriously injured the boy. Somehow I
threw my body to the left and over him, jarring my
wrist as I hit the ground. The boy stood there, quite
safe and probably never knowing how close he
was to an awful accident. I can't really count that
as a life saved though, can I? But it probably was.

**

Aircraft down
A harrier jump jet had come down not far from its
home airfield. It just happened to be close to the
boundary of three counties. In consequence,

emergency services from all three converged on the area and joined the already present RAF firefighters and rescue crews. The pilot had ejected and landed safely, and the aircraft fire was out. There was no need for any of us to be there anymore but for lack of definitive leadership by someone sharing my opinion, we were stuck there for ages.

In fact, the sooner we removed people from the area the better, and away from the possibilities of airborne carbon fibres – deadly little beasts. Most attendees never saw the downed aircraft nor had a clue as to where in the woods it was. Fire out – not our job, go home.

**

Chimney fires

Not so common nowadays, but before central heating came in, coal fires and even paraffin heaters were a regular source of heating.

We carried asbestos gloves, essentially kept dry as damp gloves just formed steam to scald the wearer, a chimney sheet or two, small sections of canvas, chimney rods with small bore hose attached and a hearth kit, a box of suitable tools for deconstructing areas around the fireplace. Along with a few cloths for cleaning and a metal bucket with a small shovel, that was it. All you needed then, was experience in doing the right thing. Difficulties arose when fires had baffles or back boilers which made rodding the chimney from below nigh on impossible.

Our options were, tackle the fire from below, above, or allow it to burn out. We went to a few roof fires caused by defective or poorly constructed chimneys, so allowing to burn out was a reluctant option . . . apart from a pub in the city where the landlord was adamant he didn't want his fire extinguished. We opted to allow it to burn out under supervision – and had a pint on the house for our troubles. So, our final option is from above, climb up on the roof and send water down. Good communication was needed and a steady hand with the water supply. The last thing we needed was a flood of sooty water all over the victim's carpet. But as you would guess, that did happen on occasions, especially if they picked the wrong chimney! We always checked the attic and any other room associated with the chimney. Spider's webs all around the chimney brickwork in the roof were seen as a good sign ... unless you were scared of spiders. On occasions, heat had cracked the chimney pot and it would need removing. I cannot imagine doing it now, nor even how I did back then, but I've stood on a frost covered slate roof ridge while hanging on to the chimney stack with one hand and dismantling the broken chimney pot with the other.

The break in. Called to a chimney fire on an old estate, we found nobody at home, but through the window could see the coal fire blazing away. The house had old metal framed casement windows and if you know how, they are easy to open without any damage. (I'll keep the secret) So we entered, spread out the protective sheet, dowsed the fire, rodded the chimney, moved the ashes outside (there was a yale lock on the door so leaving was easy) and cleaned up. The grate and surround were pristine. Cleaner than when the builders put it in. A classic and beautiful chimney job to be proud of. On my way home in the morning, I called by the house and told the elderly lady occupant what had happened. The odd thing was that she completely accepted our intrusion into her home and trusted us implicitly. That was a lovely moment. She also said, 'I thought it was strange, I was sure I'd left a good fire burning when I went out.'

One valuable thing I learned after chimney fires – always wash your hands in cold water. If you don't, then the skin pores open and fill with soot!

We could always make hot water with the hose reel pump running against closed valves. A valuable asset on a cold night. (Not for sooty hands though!)

**

Gas explosions and lightning strikes.

We attended a gas explosion at a detached house, where the occupants had been standing in the kitchen at the time and were completely unharmed, despite the french windows having been blown several metres into the back garden and a crack formed around the entire base of the building. The explosion took the path of least resistance and even left untouched, greetings cards on the mantelpiece.

There was some poor chap whose family had left him, and he attempted to gas himself, but natural gas is not the killer that the old town gas was.

However, it did explode and demolished a great deal of the house, leaving the roof perilously supported by the odd door frame. Children's toys were scattered in one of the bedrooms. I couldn't help but feel the man's pain. He had been blown out of the house onto the back lawn and though injured he survived. I often wondered if it resolved his problem, or he wished he had succeeded.

Life is not always kind.

Lightning strikes could also crack brickwork. The heat generated from the strike turned damp in the bricks to steam and explosively cracked them.

I suppose we were the lucky ones in these situations, we only attended after the event.

**

Some useful equipment I always carried with me.
Must have left it behind somewhere since those days !

**

Field fires and stubble burning laws

Field and grass fires were a common occurrence in the seventies. Mistakes were made! On occasion an appliance was driven onto a field, only to have its charred remains towed off after the fire. If we did take a vehicle onto stubble then we would wet the ground around the exhaust. Very few pumping appliances could be driven at the same time as the pump was operated. A power-take-off isolated the gearbox when the pump was in gear. I recall one field fire where we had hose reel deployed but then spotted a worse fire breaking out further along. We disconnected the hose reel at one of its joints and drove quickly to the new area, leaving the length of hose reel and its control branch behind. All I did was stick my thumb over the end to create a spray from the open hose and we quickly knocked the fire down. My station officer was incredibly impressed by such a clever move. I merely thought it was obvious.

When I moved to Cambridgeshire, they had a couple of water carriers that could pump on the move and were four-wheel drive too.

The old practice of burning straw and stubble in the fields, causing everywhere to be covered in soot smuts, choking the population and spreading fire to standing crops or elsewhere, was stopped by law. It was an unpopular move for farmers who saw the method as a way of destroying pests as well as clearing the land for new crops. On occasions 'fires were lit', and of course the fire service responded. On one occasion the senior officer who arrived to supervise proceedings, annoyed the landowner to such an extent that he was chased around the field by the incensed farmer with a pitchfork. Much to the amusement of the fire crew who watched with glee. (Perhaps even shouting encouragement. To whom?)

**

Running calls

Back in those earlier days, telephones were not as available as today, and occasionally it was quicker to run to the fire station and raise the alarm directly with the crew. They would then inform fire control that they were mobile to an incident.

At a quiet station, even a jogger coming along the road raised expectations, then disappointment as he jogged on by.

By all accounts, one day a gentleman walked into the station, introduced himself, sat down in the watch room with the on-duty crew and asked some questions. Such as, did they carry tools on the fire engines. 'Yes,' they replied, 'we have a few tools.'

'In that case,' he said, casually, 'do you think you can help my wife, she's outside in the car with her thumb trapped in the car door.'

Being at peace with the world must have been in the local's blood, for here's another. One evening an elderly gentleman called in at the station and entered into conversation with the crew. They are enjoying their chat with this nice old fellow when he finally says, 'do you think you can pop up to my house, it's on fire.' Apparently by the time they arrived the fire was so severe that the piano had dropped through the burning floor.

**

Rainstorm Rushden

Wow! Did it come down. It brought a thunderstorm with it. We were called to a barn on fire. Just filled with hay and now struck by lightning. We had to stop a couple of times on the way, once for a fallen tree, caused by the weight of rainfall and secondly because . . . the engine died. The engine cover was inside the crew cab, so we lifted it to see the engine was covered in water spray. We used our neck silks to wipe the water off the distributor cap and HT leads and the engine fired back into life. We replaced the cover and attended the barn fire. A great shame as it was a beautiful stone-built barn that eventually had to be demolished, due to severe fire damage. While we were on route we could hear many other appliances sending 'unable to continue' messages to fire control. Those were the days of petrol engines along with their coil ignition systems prone to failure in the damp. You couldn't get more damp that day. Some of our older appliances still had starting handles – and were used too!

**

Snowstorm Cambridge

'Unable to proceed' messages featured heavily on this occasion too. A heavy fall of snow had covered the county and although we could make our way around the city itself, we couldn't leave it. Abandoned cars blocked every road out of town. In the control room we listened, as appliances across the county reported that they were unable to attend their allocated incident. Control room staff were giving advice to callers over the telephone on how they might best deal with the fires themselves. Because no one was coming to help them that night.

I drove an appliance to a fire one night in falling snow, the flashing blue strobe lights froze the snowflakes in mid fall. It was quite mesmerising . . . but only briefly, as we had important places to go.

**

CS gas

I suppose I've spoiled the surprise with the title. We were called to a house with 'fumes'. There was definitely something wrong, almost like someone had burned a plastic that had left an acrid residue in the air. We vacated the premises, kept all the doors open for ventilation and sent in an observer in breathing apparatus, when he came out his exposed neck seemed red and uncomfortable. Washing it didn't seem to help him much either. Time to call in a chemical expert, and the gas company, and while we're at it, the police and ambulance too. As we were standing outside, we noticed a chap walking in large rolling, exaggerated steps in our direction and eating a bag of chips. He suddenly 'saw' us, screamed theatrically, 'oh no what can have happened,' then threw his chips and arms in the air . . . all very dramatic and ran towards our bemused crew. It turned out that earlier that day, the guy with the chips had been rifling through a language student's suitcase while he was out at college. He'd found a CS gas spray and not realising what it was, in time honoured fashion of the curious, had activated it. He visited his doctor soon afterwards. The language student knew it was illegal, so said nothing, pilfering was illegal, so the guy with the chips said nothing. They wasted a huge amount of our time and resources, but it was a good learning experience for us. And a story to tell in the pub.

**

Slum clearance.
Rows of small, terraced houses were set for clearance to build a new shopping centre. The old hostel on the corner went as well. We went there a couple of times, iron beds scattered on wooden floors, urine had burned holes through the mattress and started on the floorboards. But it was off the street, dry and sheltered. We went to a suspected fire in one of the terraces. It was used as a squat. I went up the short extension ladder to see if anyone was in. From the top of the ladder, I peered into the darkness and called out. A muffled voice answered. I called again because I couldn't work out where the voice was coming from. Much to the amusement of the crew, I was shouting in through my window and hanging out of the next and shouting back was the squatter. A strange day. No fire though.

**

Cows and other animals
From their home on the common, they used to toddle down for a drink from the river, a fairly narrow, slow flowing waterway that marked the

boundary between commons grazing and the village. Some of them either walked in or fell in. However it happened, they found themselves going for a swim, then finding themselves unable to climb the concrete bank edging. Someone would phone it in, and we would attend. Usually, we would put a line around the cow's neck and walk it along to one of the sloping access points. Makes you wonder why they couldn't find it themselves. Even if the cow looked like it was about to die, it was always prudent to remove our line from its neck before it was out of the water. Once its feet touched solid earth again, the near dead cow would spring to life and run like hell. . . . with an expensive rope necklace if we weren't careful.

It didn't always go to plan. Sometimes it depended upon how long the animal had already been in the water. Their blood shot eyes almost doing a death roll – until their feet touched ground ! One crew were guiding a cow from the far side (not a Larson's cartoon) when it suddenly turned turtle and went upside down. Realising this would not make for a good rescue, the crew hauled the cow, with only its legs above water, as quickly as they could to the near bank where they could right it. It worked, perhaps the cow held its breath or was an accomplished underwater swimmer. Either way, it lived to share its tale with the herd.

On rare occasions, the cow left the river on the wrong side, on the village side. It had been known for them to be left in people's gardens while the pinder (a person responsible for animals on the common) was summoned. They should have summoned a landscape gardener and ordered a new greenhouse at the same time!

After a cow strangled itself overnight by walking around a tree to which it had been secured, this method of capture was abandoned. Not good publicity – not so good for the cow either.

Late one afternoon our watch had a call to 'cow in river Stourbridge common.' On arrival there was no sign of the animal and dusk was beginning to fall. Then, one crew member spotted something moving in the water a couple of hundred yards downstream, 'there it is,' he called, pointing, it's swimming away from us.' This is now becoming more urgent, with darkness falling and the best access points to the river now behind them, they trudged on, following the cow, trying to catch up before it was too late. Too late arrived when the 'cow' took off. They'd followed a duck!

We came across other animals too, a gerbil in a vacuum cleaner pipe, whereby its owner was cleaning out the cage and the little fellow got sucked up and jammed, a dog down a well and a cat in a wall cavity. The strange thing is, we would spend a lot of resources releasing a pigeon from inside a stairwell, only for it to be happily shot to death by a local farmer. We could have saved him the trouble . . . but that's not good PR is it? We once spent ages trying to recapture a parrot, even to using the turntable ladder. It eventually landed on the railings of a first floor flat. As we prepared a new plan, a little old lady came out of a door and threw a towel over it. One parrot captured, at no expense. A couple of us were sent to deal with a donkey. It lived at a sanctuary but was refusing to stand up. Apparently such animals are designed to stand up, not lie down. Well, we did our best, with strops and ropes but to no avail. Later, we discovered why it was lying down, it was much older than they thought, and it had obviously thought it was a good time to die. He didn't count on the fire brigade disturbing his plan.

Cats up trees were not attended to after a fireman lost his life with a breaking branch. But, yes, there's always a but, members of the public would gather, and some would climb the tree to save the cat. Despite there being no evidence of cat skeletons littering trees and telegraph poles. Now the call is to a person in a tree, and we would respond. We would rescue the idiot, who would then promptly be hailed as the hero by an appreciative and enthusiastic cat loving crowd. We were just in the way. We should have left him up there with the cat!

Plenty of misguided people have died trying to rescue a pet that was never in any danger, and which escaped unharmed. Probably wondering where its owner had got to.

Brilliant story about a cat believed to have gone up a chimney. (Not my story, only heard about it). The crew couldn't reach the cat and decided they had to dismantle the chimney surround. They asked the old lady to go and make a cup of tea ... a ruse to take her mind off the loss of her trapped pet. After some breaking away of brickwork, one of the firemen noticed the cat lying under a chair – it hadn't been trapped up the chimney at all! Just as they heard the old lady returning with the tea, they grabbed the cat, shoved it up the chimney and rubbed it about in the soot. Just as she walked through the door, the fireman still gripping the cat pulled it out triumphantly, 'We've got him, we've got him.' They probably had their cups of tea while surrounded by building debris and one very annoyed cat.

**

Eerie silence after the bells went down.
When a 999 call came through to fire control, it rang a 'soft' bell throughout the station and hearing it we would gather in the appliance room. It was late, suspiciously there seemed to be nobody else about, but the nine's bell went, and I was straight down the pole drop into the appliance room. All was quiet there, just the low wattage night lights burning, and I could see through the control room glass that they were not taking any calls. No one else had responded. Being a suspicious chap anyway I did not go to control and ask, just in case it was a joke, with an alarm clock played over the station address system. Perhaps the crew was watching, enjoying the joke. Perhaps it was just a bell ringing in my own head. I will never know ... and we don't ask questions.

**

**

The stray dog lesson

Two of the nature loving men on our watch found a stray dog outside the station one night. Well, the excitable animal kept running about everywhere, an intolerable situation. Why not take it next door to the police station?

'It will be put down,' they said.

They tied it to the cycle shed at the far side of the drill yard, where it proceeded to do what tied dogs like to do, and with amazing endurance. It barked. It might as well have gone next door to the police pound where it could bark legally. Finally, they found a solution, and all went quiet.

In the early hours of the morning, control room staff called the 'helpful' firemen to reception to meet some people looking for a lost dog. Apparently, it wasn't their dog, they were looking after it for a neighbour, took it for a walk ... nice idea .... let it off the lead ... not so clever .... and it ran off, not returning on their command, or begging. They'd been fruitlessly searching for several worrying hours. But we know why they never found it, don't we?

They had been told by the police that the dog was at the fire station. But it wasn't, not now it wasn't, now it was fifteen miles away in a charity dog refuge. The mortified dog carers had no car, they would have to take a bus the following day to hopefully recover their neighbour's beloved pet. Did our man apologise? No. You guessed right. He simply told them off and said they should be more careful in future ... then he went back to bed.

**

Police next door

The police station was next door, we shared a wall between us. On our side, a narrow road to the outside gates, on their side, a large, caged enclosure for detaining people. Our back dormitory overlooked that area and many a time we could be amused by the desk sergeant's threats to wayward guests, 'you know what you need!'

Well, one night, when another watch was on duty, they held a drunk in the cage. He sang loudly and kept the firemen awake. In the end a guy called Steve went to the upper floor of the station, took the fire hose from its reel and poured water on to the drunk. Did it stop him singing? No, but it did change what he sang, as he entered into a spirited rendition of, 'I'm singing in the rain.' When the coppers came out to collect him later, they were probably puzzled by a drenched prisoner on an otherwise totally dry evening, not a cloud in the sky.

**

The 'monkey' officer's leaving party.

It was time to retire for the man who never took a monkey home and always had an empty desk. (I'm not bothered if this identifies him, as it's all true – and I've left out the worst of it!) He worked in a senior position at HQ. They were going to honour his service with a party. It was all set, big BBQ in the HQ's garden, colleagues gathered, gifts and speeches ready. As the time approached, they looked expectantly as he appeared in the doorway, he looked out, said, 'what a lovely day for a walk, goodbye,' and off he went, leaving some extremely surprised people to do whatever they wanted ... because that's what he was going to do!

**

Roger's story of shooting chickens

All firefighters had stories to tell. This is one of Roger's. When he was young he had friends with a farm. (Now, you can believe this or not, up to you, but I did.) The chickens ran wild, and it was easier to shoot one for dinner than try and catch it. Armed with a shotgun they set off and spotted one in front of a nettle bed. They fired but the chicken ran off, so they hunted for another. They found one and hit the mark. One dead chicken for the cook. Trouble is, on the way back, they came across the first one which had finally succumbed to its wounds. Then behind the nettle bed they found two more that had simply been in the wrong place at the wrong time. It was too risky to show the farmer four dead chickens, so they buried three and said nothing.

Had you been there to hear this tale, you would believe it too. A strange world it is eh?

**

Many a door –

Doors and firemen eh? Legalised vandalism, nothing better than kicking a door in. Always best if it is the right one though. Some houses have two front doors, one leads to stairs and the occupants of the first floor and the other to the ground floor. When there is an obvious sign of fire in the building, it's murphy's law that leads Steve to kick in the wrong one. But he's not alone, perhaps they had shares with a local carpenter. Big Vic was told to check either side of what looked like a row of empty houses, the one in the middle had a small fire. Left door in ... nothing, right side door ... a lady standing in her nightie wondering what all the noise next door was. I'm not sure who looked the most shocked. Another job for the carpenter.

We were called to a night-time fire in a bakery, the glass door was locked to us and smoke beyond the windows made it impossible to see inside. Sensibly, our man of the moment started to break the lower section of the door, minimising damage and making entry simple. As he hacked his way through the glass and started to enter, the smoke cleared a little to reveal two pairs of black shiny shoes. Policemen's shoes. They had entered the shop via the unlocked front door and stood there watching the fire brigade executing its favourite entry method. The fire was insignificant, but I bet the door cost them more than a few buns.

**

Non-emergency special services
Brigades started to charge for assisting people locked out of their homes. Firefighters weren't so money oriented and would often say, 'have you left the cooker on?' If the householder cottoned on, they might reply, 'I think I have.' It then becomes an emergency special service and there is no charge. In Cambridge, a high rise or block of flats was a rarity. One evening a chap called the brigade as he was not only locked out of his flat but out of the building. 'That's my window, there,' he pointed. A ladder was pitched, and a suitable firefighter sent aloft. As he entered the kitchen window and lowered himself down, he trod in a dish full of cat food. Probably now making a mess with every step. He made his way to the internal door release and speaker system.
'You're in,' he said, but I trod in the cat dish, sorry.'

140

'Oh dear,' said the gent, 'that's not my place, I don't have a cat!' Well, there we go then! At least he was in, out of the rain.

**

The radiation store incident

Ah, dare I tell you this? We held radioactive sources for exercises with our range of detectors and dosimeters. They were kept in a hole in the floor covered by a concrete slab in a room at the base of the drill tower. Only Station Officer rank and above were allowed the key. As a lowly leading fireman, I explained what a privilege it was for us to have the key. The two probationer firemen nodded an acceptance of the honour. When we arrived, we discovered that not only was the door not locked but nor was it properly closed. I explained how bad this was, and they nodded again. We had a quick look at the radioactive sources. No need for a lengthy examination as they were just lumps of metal busy irradiating us with nonfriendly gamma rays. Concrete cover replaced we left the small room. 'Now,' I said, 'we, are not going to leave this door unlocked, like the previous incompetent person, are we?' They nodded again, suitably impressed, I hoped. I pulled the door to close it, it jammed slightly ajar, the wood having warped. The door handle was a long vertical bar and I gripped it with both hands and gave it a heave. The screws twanged out and the handle came off in my hands. Inertia sending me

141

staggering backwards still grasping the handle to fall in perfect fit into a cut down oil drum full of spent fuel and oil. (We used them for extinguisher training) I sat in that metal tub like I was having a bath. To their credit, they did not laugh – until they were out of sight anyway. I said in my best controlled manner. 'Go and book me off the run and ask stores if they can find me some more uniform.' As I stood up, the bits that weren't soaked in dirty burnt oil, like my shoes, were soon inundated with draining liquid. Oily footprints across the drill yard showed where I was going. My clothes went in the bin, I had a shower in some stuff called 'Swarfega' – a powerful degreaser used by motor mechanics, and I ended up with some nice new uniform and a story to tell . . . or not.

**

The dead parrot's escape

Not my story, just one I heard. Urban myth? I doubt it. At a serious house fire, a little old lady asked if her parrot had survived. The Officer asked one of the crew to check.

'No, it's dead, burnt to a crisp.'

'Okay, take it out of the cage, leave the door open and drop the bird out of the window and we'll dispose of it later.'

'It's okay madam, apparently it must have escaped through the window, I'm sure it will be fine,' said the officer comfortingly. However, when she looked in the cage, the parrot's charred feet were still clinging to the perch.

**

142

'Cut off the electric!'

It just shows you the importance of good communication and training. The officer in charge of a fire wanted the electricity supply off. A fireman was sent into the basement to cut it off. After a while there was an almighty bang, and the power was off. When they went to investigate they found a shocked fireman holding a large pair of bolt cutters, the blade ends of which had disappeared, burnt off by the current when he chopped through the incoming mains cable. Lesson, always check that the person tasked, knows exactly what you mean. Thank goodness for rubber boots eh?

**

Canvas buckets

Do you see them anymore? Brilliant things. We kept a randomly filled general purpose line in one. The weight in the bucket made it easy to use as a throwing line. Easily compressible into small spaces, they could later be filled with a couple of gallons of water. (2 x 4.54 litres for metricated people). Simple, cheap, durable, with multiple uses including easily stored baler, lowering small objects in safety etc. Try and say the same about any modern piece of equipment.

We found some newts and frogs trapped in a hydrant pit once. We relocated them to a better place using a dampened canvas bucket. But not before we'd taken them on a fire call and then had dinner. Their freedom was worth the wait, I am sure.

**

Smoke travels

We were called to a very old village pub. They had discovered smoke in the first-floor rooms. With no sign of fire above, we started to investigate the boarded floor under our feet. Upon cutting and lifting part of a tongue and groove board, we discovered that they had been laid crossways on top of another set of boards. That made it even more difficult, but we cut through, making a hole big enough to look into. We found ourselves peering into a small, enclosed space. It even had ancient wallpaper still on one wall. On investigation, we found that a part of the room next to the inglenook type fireplace had been walled up. But the fire wasn't there either.

'Up the chimney?' You venture? No, though a fire was burning in the grate, there appeared nothing amiss with the surrounds. We've now followed the smoke trail as far as we can that seemed sensible. However, we eventually located the smouldering fire in the painted board cladding on the outside of the building. For whatever reason, fire had developed outside the building near to the fire place but remained hidden under cladding. If only we had known, we wouldn't have made holes in their bedroom floor. It was long before thermal image cameras and in the days when hands, eyes and nose were the detectors. Interesting little secret room though. Fortunately, no skeleton.

Unfortunately, no treasure chest either.

**

The quiet of the appliance room at night.
While the bells stay silent.

**

Whatever you can do,
or dream you can ... begin it.
Boldness has genius,
power and magic in it.

Goethe

**

The heat, so intense, no plaster left on any wall,
no wood left uncharred.
Someone's home.
Their security in life turned to ashes.

Road traffic accident instructor's course.

They gave us a demonstration of Kerie cable. Basically, oxygen is fed down a steel tube or braided steel tubing in our case. The steel is ignited and as the kerie cable burns away, the energy developed can cut through thick steel, even underwater. As the cable burns, it is obviously important to keep feeding it through your heavily gloved hands. The burning steel is chasing your hands at a fair rate ... a bit too quick for comfort. Great big, hefty leather gloves they were. We watched with interest as the instructor demonstrated. Suddenly there was wild panic. For some reason the burning steel had jumped internally, and the 'flame' appeared inside the instructor's grip. A grip he let go instantly and quickly removed the already damaged glove to inspect his hand. He was lucky indeed.

He turned to the class and asked, 'right, who wants to go first?' Nobody volunteered, and there is no doubt an excellent reason why fire and rescue services didn't buy this equipment for general use.

**

Not all errors are humorous

At a bunded fuel tank fire, a fireman was safely positioned and operating a handheld jet, all was going well. A Divisional officer arrived and knowing better, because he was a superior officer, made the man stand closer to the bund. Shortly afterwards, the wall failed and in doing so broke the fireman's leg.

147

A recall to a fire that we should have put out was embarrassing, to say the least. It was negligence, and lots of other similar and deservedly unkind words. It was something once experienced, never forgotten. We had one chap that had three recalls, one of them nearly took a whole village with it and at another, the building was lost. Not to worry though eh? He made Divisional officer rank and above. One must ask. How do they do it? Honestly, I ask you, why would you promote someone with that track record? Was he sleeping with the chief? (That last bit is obviously an alleged jest.)

**

The press
Never liked them really, they soon appeared like hyenas or vultures around the kill. The press don't operate as a social service or even behave socially responsible. They just want some sensational story to create a world of mindless gossip. Without any balanced view at all. When they wanted a photograph at a fire I would always pick a couple of firemen that had actually been in the working job, credit, were credit due. Sometimes the press would report a story that was ridiculously impossible. An example, we were parked so far from the railway shed fire that we had to use a bucket chain of fire helmets to extinguish the fire. Yes, but not from the engine, from the river only a few yards away!

One had to be very careful in their presence, they had good hearing and a knack of remembering what you said. Sneaky devils with vested interests.

148

Ramsey forty foot

Just another incident in the memory banks.

Out in the fens, the water from low lying fields is pumped into higher drainage channels that are bounded on both sides by high banks or an enclosed flood plain. Often one of the banks is used as a roadway. The roads are undulating and driving down the middle of them gives the smoothest ride. Unless someone is coming the other way of course. Never follow the loaded sugar beet lorry too closely either! The roads are straight and encourage the foolhardy or unaware to speed. The channels are usually plenty deep enough to submerge a car, some of which have only ever been found by luck. If you still have your seat belt on and the door closed when you hit the water, then it is most likely, 'goodnight Vienna.' Every year, cars ended up in the water, the steep slope down to the surface preventing steering out of the situation. Fire crews would bravely do their best but inevitably too late. Two brave chaps who had entered the water to try and save the driver were saddened by their failure, they were soaked and cold. The benefit of having my car there was I had a spare tunic and a track suit in the boot. They returned them neatly washed and dried, with thanks. To even be a tiny part of the great team is satisfying indeed.

Often they were local people, the crews would know the victim. Driving slower saves lives. We know that, so why don't we?

Near the village of Mepal, the difference between farmland and the necessary height of the drains is clear to see. The river changes flow with the tide.

**

Civil defence, readying for Armageddon

After the disbandment of the Civil Defence force, we were still engaged in the 'cold war'. They set up a new group called Civil Protection and recruited Community Advisers. These were the people who would guide communities after the bomb dropped. About as useful as the 'Protect and Survive' campaign that told people how to build a shelter in their homes but forgot to explain the reason. It kept bodies off the street and neatly buried them under the soil they used for their shelter. Still, we can live in hope! The advisers needed training and the designated emergency planning officer who was seconded to the Home Office, complete with own budget, wasn't that keen to do it. As I enjoyed training so much, I got the job. It was paid overtime that didn't contradict union rules as it came from the Home Office budget.

It was interesting, to say the least, and using some appalling quality and ancient Civil Defence documents, I worked my way through the syllabus of ladders, knots and various other basics. Fire Service humour was dangerous with them. When I said we should be more wary of the Americans than the Russians, one lady told me her husband was American. Not only that, but she was having help with knots and lines from a neighbour – who turned out to be the brigade's third officer. Whoops! She called him, 'Frank', I called him, 'Sir', (we'll meet him again later at the reservoir). We made use of an old civil defence building that still stood and was full of the sort of constructions you might find after a bomb had hit. It included a brick wall that had deformed shapes and mock cracks built in.

The irony is that we later discovered a couple of genuine cracks in the brickwork, and as a result we were never allowed to use it again. Training for nuclear catastrophe stopped in its tracks by the danger of a splinter.

I left 'A' frame training until the end, while I tried to discover what it was!

**

Peat fires

Hard to believe, but some farmers didn't seem to care as their land burned away. Don't you find that odd? Our brigade used to supply them with equipment to extinguish their own fires, which had usually been started by them anyway. Peat fires can be incredibly dangerous, they can burn under roadways, and they can burn deep enough to lose a bus. The burned peat ash holds its structure but not its strength. So, a burned peat pit looks no different until you step on it and fall into the hot ash some distance down. The only way to extinguish the fire is with hard hitting jets or metal tubes that can be pushed deep underground. It is useless only hitting the surface fire. The fire shown in the photographs was only tackled by the brigade because the residents of Ely were down wind and suffering from weeks of incessant and unpleasant smoke. There was a river nearby, so we set light portable pumps into open water and ran jets off them. We had a thermal image camera at training centre, I took it with me and observed the hot spots in the field. With a simple map drawn up on a sheet of paper we could circle the locations requiring attention. The system worked well, though it took a few days to complete the job. The farmer would have let it burn forever. I still cannot understand why. Madness.

Not easy to find the hot spots and not easy to
extinguish them either.
Peat fires can burn or smoulder for months. Coal seams
can burn underground for years.

**

153

Embarrassing fires to attend.

Shame on us. However, I was only a fireman at this factory fire, I was not in charge of driving the fire through the building. Instead of gaining access where the fire could be held and stopped, we entered where the fire started and drove it all the way through. Result is clearly seen in the photo.

According to one of the crew, they had done the same to a previous industrial building fire. They say, firemen burn all their mistakes. Pity they didn't learn from them. Anyone wishing to take issue with this might like to explain why it was that fire discoloured coins appeared on the station shortly afterwards. Embarrassing isn't the right word, shame is. Betrayal of trust is an evil thing. Now that was a skill the officers in charge had in spades. There are many truths that they will never want aired.

Back to the fire though, and my part in its journey. I was inside, in breathing apparatus with a colleague, and we had a jet to work. Above and all around us was racking holding burning materials of unknown source. Our jet hit the main switch gear and the place lit up with electrical arcing. We moved the jet away immediately and reported the fact that the electricity was still on. We were told, 'well go and turn it off then!' That's right, we were going to do that, weren't we? With soaked hands and tunics, we were expected to grope in the dark to find a suitable switch to isolate the factory. And we'd just seen how it reacted to water. It would have been certain death .... so, we didn't.

While we stood together in the dark with the jet, we could hear a hissing noise from nearby. I joked with my colleague, because we couldn't possibly smell anything with our masks on, 'Can you smell gas?' I don't recall his answer. As we ran low on air, we were replaced and removed our sets in fresh air. My colleague, who was senior in service to me, said, 'come on, let's take a walk, we have done our bit for the moment.' So, we had a brief walk in the fresh air alongside the building, then returned to see a group of firemen carrying an acetylene cylinder out of the building to place it in a cooling dam. (In fact, experienced firefighters might argue with how they dealt with that too.) So, the hissing noise we had heard was the gassing off sound of a highly heated acetylene cylinder. Had it burst and not gassed off, putting the fire out would have been the least of our worries. Such officers were never to be trusted, I certainly never trusted them ever again. And it wasn't only this one fire either. They must have had deluded friends in high places. If you were picking a team, they would never feature on your list. Guaranteed.

The unnecessary result of poor fire command.

**

Posh furniture and cakes

Out in one of the villages, crews had battled a fire in a furniture warehouse. Damage was fairly severe, and one firefighter was taken to hospital having had a hot nail go through the side of his boot. The fire was out, but in case anything should go wrong they sent a crew to stay overnight on a watching brief. We parked up and settled in. In the early hours, the bakery next door was in full swing and a quick visit to purchase a snack ended up in the gift of a few cakes, and very nice they were too. Clad in our warm fire kit, we sat on the posh furniture in the semi darkness, lovely furniture it was, much of it with red leather and brass studs. We ate our cakes and rested in the smoke scented air, while over us, bits of hanging damaged roofing swayed in the cool breeze, the night sky clear above us through the gaps. It was a lovely night out. As dawn broke, we were relieved by a lone fireman with the water carrier. More importantly he had brought with him the makings of fried breakfasts for all. A grand night out, by anyone's account, surely.

**

Relief crews in four hours?

At a hard-working job it was normal to be relieved with fresh crews every four hours. We worked our socks off on this thatch fire, secured the furniture from within and created a fire break in the thatch roof. Much of it simply torn out by strong hands. We were exhausted, sweat started to go cold in our wet uniforms, we'd had no break, no relief. The officer in charge, who had done nothing of any practical use all evening, being the same officer who oversaw the wrong doors being installed on a station's garages and a few other things like the smoke detector debacle, made the generous decision that, as we had nearly finished, it would be silly to drag a fresh crew out from their comfy station. So, we had to keep at it until all was done. Then make up all our gear, return to station, refuel, clean dirty stuff, change the hose etc and dig out our dry replacement uniform. We were good for nothing else that night, we were knackered. I don't suppose he was though, off home to bed no doubt.

157

A crew member cuts away the wire mesh so we can remove the thatch.

In the first photo, you can see the dormer window gives a more level platform to work from. A colleague, in a misguided feat of skill, jumped from there onto another part of the roof. There were consequences. The main roof being much steeper and still covered in wet and slippery wire mesh. His feet went from under, and he slid as gracefully as his surprised bulk would allow, into the garden below. There waiting for him, a spiked railing fence. However, his luck was in. We had removed so much thatch already that he had a safe, if embarrassing, landing and climbed back up the ladder to join us.

**

Old Addenbrookes hospital - power off

I seem to remember it was due to an electrical storm. I was in the control room when the call came in. I used to enjoy being there with them as they answered calls from all over south Cambs. Once they had a call from London fire brigade. A local Chinese restauranteur couldn't speak any English and had called his pal in London who dialled 999 and explained.

I digress, if I remember the occasion rightly, the on-call officer who should have responded to make decisions couldn't make it as his wife was frightened of thunder. Not very helpful for the surgeon doing an eye operation at the old hospital. Their power had gone off and they needed help.

One of the old hands in control did just that, he admirably took control, and mobilised us to the incident, only a minute or so from the station. We were to take all available spare lighting, torches, search lights, you name it. The police and the military from a nearby Royal Engineers' unit also attended with what they could muster. Fortunately, it wasn't too long before power was restored to the area.

Why didn't they have an emergency generator? Oh, they did.

Why didn't it work then?

Oh, it worked fine, except that it was wired up back to front ready to supply power in the wrong direction.

Why didn't they test it?

Perhaps it is difficult to turn off all the power at an operational hospital. The hospital also ran on a strange voltage, no normal equipment would work in there without a transformer. It's one more reason why they built a new hospital I suppose.

**

Rustled cattle

Some enterprising thieves thought they might make a killing on the meat market and somehow managed to rustle some young bovine beasts. They used a furniture removal van for the deed. It didn't go well; something must have gone terribly wrong as they had to abandon the effort. The beasts were left free to roam and had been carefully rounded up by staff from the experimental farm. Yes, that's right - experimental. However, they had one problem, one of their beasts was stuck in a ditch. That's the bit when they called us. I decided to put in an assistance call for our turntable ladder – to use as a crane. Something rarely done but quite within its remit. I ended up with a senior officer as well, but only because he was curious as to why we wanted a crane for a cow. It went to plan and luckily the beast was already knackered. The still cautious handlers warned us to be very careful as this animal was bred from Spanish fighting bull stock. There's a lesson for all rustlers, make sure you know what it is you are nicking.

**

Hostile crowd

It was a house fire and going well by the time a fire crew arrived. A couple of dogs died in the blaze and the crowd outside were cursing the brigade for taking so long to turn up. When asked, 'who called the fire brigade?' There was a stony silence, not one of them had.

**

Polystyrene ceiling tiles

They were very popular at one time, a cheap and cheerful way of insulating and covering cracked ceilings. They ceased in popularity when it became obvious that they added to the fire loading of the room and helped burn a few places down. Although, in one instance, we attended a single room fire where all the polystyrene tiles had melted and dropped in the fire and yet the fire had smothered itself. The average living room only has enough oxygen to burn two bags of sugar. Even the fish in the aquarium were unaffected by what to them must have been an intriguing sight. No human would have survived, we are much alike, fires and us, we both need to breathe.

**

Hazmat and radiation

I trained as a hazmat/radiation officer, but I suspect my efforts were all in vain. The idea was to have two trained officers, one to go to the scene and the other to fire control. From their respective positions and with identical training and shared knowledge, they should be able to deal with the situation. My 'fellow officer', of senior rank, never even acknowledged my presence. My suspicion is that he was not up to the job, otherwise he would have spoken to me about how he saw our roles. In an earlier life I had worked in laboratories and was qualified to HNC in Chemistry. I had also retained a keen interest in that aspect of fires. Based on my learning at Moreton I designed some useful algorithms. Nice easy tick sheets for use at an incident. They ended up in the bin, like me.

**

Radio masts.

Not ours, (ours were the ones that CB radio enthusiasts used to broadcast under, to boost their signal, and in consequence obliterated fire service radio communications). No, these masts were more modern and owned by private companies, not ancient home office stuff. In their wisdom, the management, sold the space on the top of our drill towers to private contractors.

Orders were rapidly issued.

'There is <u>absolutely no danger</u> from the new radio masts on drill towers. However, any station so fitted must <u>under no circumstances</u> allow any personnel within one floor of an operational mast.'

Nice one. Really useful management of resources. I mean, what is a drill tower for? Making money?

**

Station's rear garage doors

The brigade must have come into some cash, as they decided to replace still quite serviceable wooden doors with modern concertina metal ones. The back garages were extensive, we used parts for breathing apparatus training and the station stored various specialist or reserve vehicles. A senior officer with the presumed necessary skills was designated to oversee the project. On occasions he could be seen measuring and supervising. Some of the free redundant wood was utilised by another officer to make bat boxes. The new doors were superb, painted in a glorious red and sliding effortlessly in their runners. 'Beautiful job,' he must have thought. 'Okay, time to hand it over to the station.'

It's a good thing that no vehicles were left in the garage while work was undertaken – or they'd still be stuck in there. The top runners, required for the new concertina doors, had lowered the door height so much that fire appliances could no longer fit in. One wonders how they can live with the shame afterwards, but they seem to manage okay.

**

Snow plough

The garages could however house things like the snow plough. Yes, that's right, a snow plough. Great big heavy thing it was, as evidenced by the way it adversely affected the steering of the water carrier that it would be attached to, as and when required. The water carrier being the only four-wheel vehicle we had of sufficient power.

Did we ever use it? No, of course we didn't. Mainly because when the plough was attached, it covered the headlights, and the driver couldn't see where he was going. This wasn't the idea of a mere divisional officer, no, this was a top guy, a senior DO and head of the department that worked on such useful projects. Aren't some of these things obvious to at least someone, somewhere along the way? Preferably before the job is painted red and finished.

**

The training centre - methods

I used to watch the recruits lined up in the drill yard by the fire appliance, rigged in fire kit and waiting for the supervising officer to appear. There is no doubt they were under a lot of pressure. They were expected to perform at speed and with competence meanwhile subject to our favourite

164

pastime of being shouted at above the roar of the racing diesel engines and whining pumps. One particular officer made them twitch nervously the moment he appeared, striding purposefully in their direction. He would shout in each of their faces, asking a question. 'Name of the third officer. Quick man!' I used to think, 'not sure I know some of the answers and I'd been there years.

I decided that I would adopt a more friendly student-centred approach. It would work in my favour as well as theirs. What did I need them to do? Well, perhaps pitch a ladder without too many errors. So, I would gather them, without shouting, around the ladder and we would slowly walk through what each position on the ladder would mean should they be assigned that place. Each stage would be explained, and each student would be sure of the task. Running through the drill repeatedly and slowly gaining speed and confidence was a far better way of teaching and learning. It became a pleasure for all concerned.

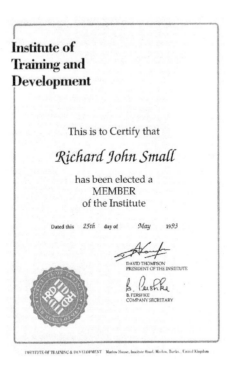

Institute of
Training and
Development

This is to Certify that

Richard John Small

has been elected a
MEMBER
of the Institute

Dated this   25th   day of   May   1993

DAVID THOMPSON
PRESIDENT OF THE INSTITUTE

B. PERSHKE
COMPANY SECRETARY

INSTITUTE OF TRAINING & DEVELOPMENT   Marlow House, Institute Road, Marlow, Bucks., United Kingdom

I joined the ITD, it was a fantastic organisation. There were frequent meetings where trainers displayed their wares. What was so good about them was that a trainer cannot let their audience go, not until they had learned something useful. The ITD sold their soul to amalgamate with the Institute of Personnel Management. Then meetings became no different to the stale mould prevalent within the management by my own superior (senior) officers. With its very life snuffed out by indifference and stifling inaction. Our heroes were subjugated to morbidity. (In my opinion.)

166

Whilst the profile may be accurate in terms of 'reviving' processes it is should not be seen as a reflection of the product — your 'performance' capability was <u>excellent</u> at outset.

Your enquiring and investigative approach was found to bring about changes perceptible in yourself but barely perceptible to external observers since it merely varies in <u>shades of</u> excellence

The final profile is certainly more like the highly competent and capable person seen at all times on course. I feel sure your ability to put a course together is exceeded by none !! As is true of your ability to execute and deliver

Complimentary comments by the senior lecturer at college about stages of my studies in further and adult education. Spot on, brilliant judge of character !

My colleagues in the training centre amusingly embellished my photo. (Well, I think they did it as a joke, but, who knows, perhaps not.) In some ways it pleased me to think that they thought I was that capable, but then, what else did they think? Anyway, I've kept the photo, for the fun I hope that they had too.

We didn't adopt SS tactics in our training – for a start we weren't issued with smart leather coats and lugers and our only interest was for students to leave a course better equipped to meet the real world.

Just an aside on what people call the 'real world'. The real world is not some mythical place outside, the real world is right where you are now. Right this minute, regardless of what you are doing. This is still your reality.

I so enjoyed working at the training centre, rewriting or developing lectures, the practical work in ladders, pumps and breathing apparatus too. Watching recruits progress through their five-day training, and more often than not succeeding with competence, was rewarding. To stop the station personnel playing any tricks on them, for it was a residential affair with them sleeping on the lecture room floor, one of the instructors would spend a night on the office floor. Sort of night watch nanny!

They were the happy days.

Where it all went wrong was in our management.

**

'The wise man leads you
not to enter the house of his own wisdom
but leads you to the threshold of your own learning.'

Kahlil Gibran

**

Hose out of control training.

169

To recapture a high-pressure jet with snaking hose, we taught that two firefighters would crawl along the hose, gradually controlling it as they went, then as a team to stand and direct the jet safely. I must have had an aberration one day because I forgot that bit and demonstrated the technique on my own. I thought it was a bit awkward. Still, we all make mistakes. This was just one of mine.

Apart from basic courses we also ran a 3rd year course, during which we tried to give the crews some interesting and challenging experiences not normally possible with on station training. We'd take them to a local animal sanctuary to gain insights into dealing with animals in difficult circumstances. (Another of my ideas. I never made a fuss about my contribution while working but don't see why I should avoid the credit forever. There were plenty that took advantage at the time.) There were all sorts of interesting adaptions to make with ladders. Bridging ladders as per the drill book and bridging ladders in even more clever ways . . . definitely not in the book. Ladders can be used on steep slopes as steps or crossing ditches or gaps between buildings, short extension ladders in conjunction with salvage sheets can be used to create dams to hold water. We made step ladders out of extension ladders too, and in general tried to make the course an enjoyable and eye-opening experience. It was possible to pitch a ladder to an upper window then place a short extension ladder between that and the next lower window cill. Tied off, of course. I had done this before and it did, I am quite sure, appear somewhere in very old fire manuals. However, my training colleague refused to carry out my instructions. 'I'm not doing that,' he said, 'we could kill someone.'

I thought, 'yeah, but if they don't die they will go back to stations with wonderful memories.' However, he was right, and we didn't carry out that particular drill. We will never know if someone would have fell to their deaths and caused lots of paperwork or achieved it successfully and dined out on the story for life. Better safe than sorry and I had a lot of trust and respect in my colleague. (Still do Les.)

**

The cartoon appears

We had a new officer in charge of Cambridge station. He arrived at the same time as a cartoon appeared on the locker room notice board. There was a uniformed man with short spiky hair, sitting at a desk. It did vaguely resemble our man.

The caption read, 'Two days ago I couldn't even spell stashun officah, and now I are one.'

Although it was removed fairly quickly, obviously the instigator had lots of copies, so it became a regular and amusing feature of the locker room.

**

Smoke detector campaign.

I spent six months working on a smoke detector campaign. We had a huge store of two different makes of detector, both using a small radioactive source. The plan, (not mine), was to invite the public to request a visit by myself for advice on siting. All pensioners were given a free detector. A couple of things went wrong, well lots of things really. I was inundated with requests on application forms carrying their details. So, first thing, contact them, – that's if they were in. Next arrange a mutually convenient time for the visit. Going through the list in order and having appointments that could be many miles apart made the logistics burdensome to say the least. However, I plodded on and had great success on each individual visit. Then I had a visit myself, from the man in charge, (our friend who wouldn't ask for reliefs at four hours and measured the doors wrong) who wanted to know if it could all be completed in a given time frame. Well, 'no', was the answer, they had opened a can of worms by inviting the whole county to apply and it looked like it would take years to accomplish. Perhaps they hadn't factored in the time it took to drive to a remote village and then return after spending at least 30 minutes with the client. It could easily take a morning for each one. He wasn't best pleased as he'd already given the chief, the 'don't worry guv, I've got this. The war will be over by Christmas,' speech. All change and, panic. All the flexible duty officers were tasked with picking up some appointments. They loved doing it as it was on mileage and a doddle. They made a fortune on mileage claims whereas I had been told to use only brigade transport, anything available, car from fire prevention dept, van from workshops or the station, in fact anything but my own vehicle. I was very lucky a couple of times, after a lengthy and exhaustive, time robbing search for a vehicle, there were none and I used my own car. In six months, I made about £6. The detectors we gave to the elderly were often defective and required more time stealing revisits to replace them. It became obvious to me that the make we were giving away had faults and I left a report on my senior officer's desk. I was called in later to be informed that the note was in the bin and if I ever mentioned it again I would be on a discipline charge. That's life eh?

Last thing about the campaign. We employed a neighbour of one of the officers to handle the extensive admin required to process hundreds of applications. I noted that there was an error in the balance between what we once had and the current stock. It looked like we were missing some detectors. I pointed to the discrepancy on her documents. Once she finally understood what I meant, she fixed it. She merely crossed out some numbers, wrote in some new ones . . . and hey presto the lost detectors came back. On paper only. Still, she was the boss's neighbour and I'd made enough enemies by then and with luck I'd be back on an operational watch soon. The bit I liked about the campaign, was meeting some lovely people and helping them, that was the joy of it. Nothing else.

**

Being part of the watch

It was great, we were all individuals but when called to account, we were a team. Whatever the problem, we would stand together and be confident in each other. Thinking about that, it is one of the greatest honours, that others will see you as worthy to stand alongside them in the face of danger. Each knowing they could trust the other with their life. On occasion, some members of the watch would get together for an outing. Once we went to Blythe to visit the Breathing Apparatus manufacturer. Eight of us stopped overnight at the fire station. we slept on the station beds .... only god knows where the night shift went, but they were there for breakfast. On the way home we met a snowstorm, I was driving as fast as was possible, which was fortuitous as the A1 road was blocked by snow later that night. I joked, 'I don't know about you,' I said, ' but I can't see a thing.'

To which the worried front seat passenger shouted, 'well slow down then!' The two in the back picked up on the joke and demanded I drove faster as they wanted to be home for tea.

We would also engage in long distance walks, many organised by the west midlands.

Every visit carried its story into the future. Enough for many books. It always felt like the watch you were on was the best one. There is so much that could be said, so much.

Menin gate Ypres

I travelled with one colleague to stay with a Fireman in Lille. Max the Sapeur Pompier. From there we visited Ypres and the fire station. It is the fire service bugler that sounds the last post at the Menin Gate. A huge structure engraved with the names of those they never found after the battles. An emotive place and an inspiring moment as the bugle echoes down the street. Another enduring

175

link with fellow firefighters. We were the same the world over, as I discovered on visiting a fire station in Jerusalem. Or dropping into Wolverhampton station for assistance on my way home from a long walk. (Short on fuel with no money, they fed me and lent me some cash. – Returned with interest of course.)

Camaraderie, the 'watch spirit'.
The three peaks walk, Yorkshire.

We enjoyed quite a few off-duty events together.

Wide awake – immediately

It is amazing how sensitive you become to certain sounds, especially when they are linked to a surge of adrenalin. At Cambridge station, kind control staff would put the lights on first before the bells. Because there were so many lights operated by one switch, they had to be connected to a relay. The gentle click of the relay was enough to have us wide awake before the lights and bells were fully operational. There was no need to stretch, yawn, blink or any of the normal waking up procedures. No. Bang. You were wide awake and fighting fit in a flash, ready to slide down the pole drop into the waiting appliance room.

I became just as sensitive to my pager and telephone. There was, however, a downside. It was a habit you couldn't switch off. I recall being on holiday in a B&B and for some reason the alarm clock went off in the early hours of the morning. In an instant I was standing in darkness by the bed, trying desperately to work out where I was. Sleep is neither easy nor good for you after an adrenalin fix. At one time, my ex-wife asked if I would like to buy an electric alarm clock from her. (A free gift from some shopping catalogue I think.) I gave her a tenner for it, took it home, plugged it in and set it for a suitable morning awakening. If I tell you that such a device was probably similar to the warning klaxon on a nuclear submarine, you might just have some idea what it was like. I only used it once and gave it back. Terrifying noise it made, no wonder it was a free gift.

Hospital visits

Perhaps I was born with a good measure of empathy, I don't know, but for whatever reason behind my actions, I always visited firefighters that had been hospitalised. Even as a junior officer on the watch I would drive many miles in the opposite direction to home in order to visit a sick or injured colleague. I always thought that was a decent thing and the very least we should do. I thought that was part of our job, part of our duty to care. Don't you? I've also done my bit talking to the unconscious in hospices too. Being aware that hearing is the last to go, gives us hope that we might share some last reassuring words to those facing the unknown.

I have myself, known what it is like to lose all senses but hearing. It gave me an insight into the possibilities for others.

As for lost colleagues, some not with us for many years now, I still see them sometimes in my dreams. Often they are well, happy and tell me they are doing alright. Occasionally someone will appear in a dream and, upon waking, I wonder why on earth I had seen them. Someone not well known and not seen for over twenty years, but there they are, playing a part in some subconscious story. Other times it might be a respected colleague who has turned up to help me with an overwhelming task, or just to smile as they carry a tray of rinks in a pub and say, 'I'm doing okay, I'm in the garden with friends.'

I'll leave it there to my own memories.

Are they ghosts? Or are they just dreams?

Lots about boats now

Grafham Water is the 3ʳᵈ largest reservoir in England. It's ten miles to circumnavigate.

One of our 'little boats' at Grafham Water

Some basic training was given by a senior officer - his qualification was that he once had a yacht.
In fact, it wasn't bad. We looked at towing methods and man overboard reactions. He was a good bloke. The two images above and below are on the tidal Nene and taken from the local station's twin 40 HP dory.

Firefighters are often masters of amusing understatement. If you fell in the river, a sign would appear on the station notice board that Fireman X was available to give swimming lessons. Or, like when a good colleague fell from a height through a damaged roof on to burning straw, (He was really lucky with that one. The burning straw had formed a slope down which he rolled to safety and just walked out as though nothing had happened) a note soon appeared that free advice on parachuting was available courtesy of Fireman P white watch.

While being 'trained' on our small inflatable boats, I was sitting on the sponson (inflated tubes) when the knowing instructor, the officer who'd had a yacht, made a calculated turn. The movement took my weight backwards and there was nothing to grip hold of. In consequence I rolled slowly off the boat and into the reservoir. Long enough to hear him clearly and calmly ask with theatrical curiosity, 'why are you getting out?'

As if he didn't know!

Lesson learned and still alive . . . if somewhat wet.

*

Setting up a tow for a boat larger than your own.
Retaining control over the lines for security.
When their boat sinks,
you don't want yours going with it!

**

Ahoy there! - Boat load of chickens.

That evening inside Ye Olde Worlde village pub, my old work colleague vigorously and almost demonically, bounced on the wooden bench seat, 'boing, boing, boing,' went Dick; crack, crunch, snap went the bench. He was suddenly silent and still, and somewhat sheepish; a lot

182

different from his earlier alcohol fuelled bravado and jollity.

What brought this about? I'll tell you …… if you have but a minute.

It starts with a bad manager we once shared. You may well have suffered at the hands and mind of such a creature yourself.

It went a bit like this.

Stage 1: deny any useful staff the chance to go on a course, especially if it looks like being good fun.

Stage 2; make sure your own name is included on the course list.

3; having been on the course, had a free meal and claimed mileage, never ever put your new skills into use.

4; realise that you need someone to carry out all the work that you don't want to do.

5; select a couple of the originally ignored 'useful people', (they'll catch up, won't they?)

6; don't send them on the beginner's course, there's no time for that now – as you've already left it too late. Send them on the advanced course instead. ('Not done the basic course? Oh, it was so easy; you don't need that silly one first.')

7; expect gratitude from the selected staff you are now belatedly sending.

8; ensure that you tell your own boss that all is under control now – thanks entirely to your omnipotent and invaluable forward-thinking inimitable self, of course.

Dick and I were the chosen 'useful' ones and the day of the course duly arrived – a boating course it was to be precise, power-boating all the way to fleet rescue level. Yup, from 'yes, I understand that thing there is a boat', to highly skilled manoeuvres and lifesaving procedures carried out with speed and precision under any conditions.

Dick and I were sent along to a local RYA training establishment in the County, where we introduced ourselves to Bob, a likeable and highly competent 'boat person'. Even with all his skills and experience, he looked a little shocked and indeed bewildered as we answered his question on our previous boating experience, which, note, he expected to be considerable, ... 'Well, we've seen a boat, does that count?' ... 'I've been on the Dover ferry a couple of times', 'what do you mean by; 'it's a RIB?'

'Oh, well', Bob sighed, 'we'll just do our best and see what happens; come on let's get some buoyancy aids – we must be careful – you can die out there.'
'Not good news for a chap that can only swim the length of his bath,' I thought, as I donned a buoyancy aid that didn't look hardly big enough to aid itself.

The deep and toxic blue-green algae contaminated reservoir is over 2 miles long and a strong south westerly wind had whipped up some good-sized waves into a frenzy along its entire length. We stood on a heaving wave lashed jetty, (a floating pontoon), next to which, straining on its mooring line, rocked a five-metre-long grey inflatable boat with central seating for two and powered by a 50 HP motor; rising spray obliterated any chance of seeing the opposite bank.

Bob said to me, 'Right, in you get; this coiled red plastic cable is the 'kill cord' (ominous name that eh?), put it on every time you drive the boat, if you go overboard it stops the engine and you might stand a chance of re-boarding without losing a limb, make sure you steer with your left hand and control the engine power from the throttle with your right hand - *got that*?'.

The three of us had a slow dawdle in semi sheltered water near the jetty. 'OK,' Bob said, 'now swap over, let me off the boat, I'll be back down here soon. Take the boat out but *don't go too far.*'

As Bob left us to walk away up the hill to the boat centre; *(He'd probably gone to check his desk for alcohol, Valium or steroids, or perhaps all three!)* Dick took the controls, and, in one deft and foolhardy move, he was flat out going dead ahead, downwind, throttle wide open and both hands clamped firmly to the steering wheel and, as though relishing the wild weather, he bounced us from wave to wave. Our boat and novice crew were soon engulfed by wind born spray and wave troughs somewhere in the centre of a grey green hell.

Now, I have to confess that I suffered a modicum of some stuff they call in the trade, 'fear', but not wishing Dick to realise this I merely shouted above the wind, racing engine and the crash of the boat on wave tops, and as nonchalantly as a petrified non swimmer in a maelstrom can, 'not too far Dick, …. Bob said, *not too far!*'

185

For a brief moment he glanced behind and with a typically polite yet smug attitude, he roared with almost pleasurable derision, *'Chicken!'*

Can you imagine, you are pillion riding a boat heavily battered by waves and soon to be battered even harder by the fast-approaching concrete dam wall, and your driver turns out to be a power crazed looney.

Dick eventually slowed the boat and we turned to head back towards the jetty, ... what jetty? All we could see was white wave tops, (the ones you never see when going down wind). We headed back, soundly thrashed by wind and spray, and now even more pummelled as we met the waves head on, all the way to a waiting jetty and Bob.

We said nothing. Bob said nothing.

Several years later in this pub, Dick finally confessed that he'd been trying to slow down all along but that each time he took his hand off the wheel to adjust the throttle we hit a wave and his hand instinctively retreated to the seemingly relative safety of the steering wheel. It was his excitable and detailed re-enactment of the event that brought about the demise of the pub bench; at least we could only drown our sorrows in there.

Still, at last – we had a confession, and the truth was out – a boat full of chickens.

PS. The chickens survived to both become powerboat instructors ..... After a bit more practice

The **powerboat instructor's course** was all you might think it is ... intense, educational, rewarding, character building, inspiring and exciting. As well as enjoying the company of like-minded colleagues. One thing does stick in my mind, the painted over glasses that we were made to wear on certain tests, so we couldn't see where we were going. We were two up in two boats, 5m RIB or Dory, each driver was 'blindfolded' and had to take instructions from his sighted companion. Good communication at all times is a byword in boating, and we certainly needed it then as we were instructed to take our boats at speed around a course as well as slower manoeuvres like mooring to buoys . . . meanwhile avoiding the other boat. It was quite amazing how accurate a boat could be driven with the right skills and correct guidance.

There is a wonderful manoeuvre for coming alongside a jetty at speed. In fast at a narrow angle, then just before hitting the jetty, turn the wheel into shore and a hard blip on the throttle in reverse. The boat stops parallel to and just kisses the jetty. Talk about elation on achieving such a move, absolutely great. We did all the usual stuff too, rescues from the water, transferring crew from one boat to another at speed. I bet you want to have a go now, don't you?

I'd love to do it again, but age is definitely against success. Success in being able to walk again after only an hour in the boat!

I have a number of photographs from boat courses, because it was a training, and not an operational, situation. I was always pleased with the efficiency and effort put in by the firefighters on these courses.

People you could really be proud of and trust.

**

A desperate lee shore rescue drill, always challenging,
Here a crew's sheer determination wins through.

Lee Shore Rescue

Six they were, standing in smart dark-blue uniform, all gathered attentively in the appliance room of a mid county fire station.

'This is what you will be using,' said the instructor to the firefighters as they assembled around the three-metre-plus red inflatable boat. 'This is how it is inflated, please all have a go,' he continued.

Here is the equipment we must carry, and it should all be secured inside the boat . . . just in case it flips over . . . we don't want to lose valuable equipment, do we?'

They laughed, but land lubbers all, the thought of the boat possibly capsizing was a new one on them. So far, their only watery excursion, officially that is, had been lifejacket training. It was carried out in full fire kit, including boots and breathing apparatus – good fun it had been, self-rescue, partner rescue, cold water entry and the rare and normally banned use of breathing apparatus underwater. Banned because it wasn't designed or certified for such application. It took part in an indoor heated swimming pool at a classy sports club. Not quite the same as the cold and murky, sixty foot (20 m) deep waters of the local reservoir they would visit later that week.

'Right, nearly time for lunch, make all the gear up and load it in the van ready for this afternoon's practical,' said the instructor.

It was amazing how quickly they could get to work when a dinner was waiting.

They loved courses did the firefighters, something new to learn, a chance to work with colleagues from other stations or watches – plus – meals were provided free for all students. Let's hope nobody would be seasick!

Lunch over and keen to go, they left early for the river only a couple of hundred yards from the station. There they found the convenient slipway and car park as well as a firm grass launching bank aside the calm and lazy water. Boats inflated, launched and all gear stowed, the heavy 10HP outboards were handed over to the crews afloat. Everyone had a go, forward, reverse, fast and slow, coming alongside, changing crews, coxswain in charge and crew on lookout. (For trees, shopping trolleys and anything else in their way.)

The week moved on, as did their skills. Man-overboard drills – not with real people mind you, approach to weirs and sluices and so much more. They were becoming proficient and quite comfortable with all the gear, though this particular course did have a little trouble with anchoring.

They'd lost two anchors so far, in fact the line that held the anchor was surprisingly more expensive than the four-pronged metal bit at the heavy end! One was lost when it became inextricably hooked on an immovable object on the lake floor and another when thrown overboard. The crew watched the metal bit disappear into the depths followed by the anchor line ... then the end of that too ... an unsecured end! Nothing to see but murky water. Gone. 'Whoops,' was the combined silent thought of all present. Accidents are bound to happen; no omelette was ever made without the ritual sacrifice of the odd egg or two.

Time was of the essence – we had one day left to go and the weather was turning against us. Beaufort scale four was the limit for our boats, that's up to eighteen miles per hour winds, that would bring white horses to the waves across the reservoir.

Lee shore rescue – what does it take?

It was the last day of the boat course, the instructor was pleased with his students. All had been hardworking, never daunted, ever willing and achieved all that was asked of them. What more could he ask than that?

All were strong, fit and young firefighters, probably none would ever have thought that when they joined they would be dealing with water borne risks and handling boats for search, rescue and firefighting purposes.

They'd come a long way from the warm indoor swimming pool and lifejacket training – further than you might think. Fit the activation cylinder in the jacket wrongly and it wouldn't work. (In my opinion, a design flaw.) Put the lifejacket on before the breathing apparatus and when inflating it would not only squeeze your ribs but not expand enough to give secure floatation. Ah, so much to learn and to do right first time in an emergency. The heavy outboard motor seemed to become lighter with practise, as did the 3.8 metre red inflatable. It was warming to see how quick they could assemble everything they needed, inflate and launch their two craft.

They'd learned how to take command as coxswain and control the boat in varying conditions, sluice gates, man overboard, coming alongside, anchoring and towing both larger and smaller vessels.

As the last day, it was a chance to test their skills further, on advanced tasks unlikely to be met in future but none the less would equip them to react swiftly and with certainty on anything similar.

Lee shore rescue – when the wind is blowing towards the shore it makes an approach with the rescue craft all the more difficult. It can easily become a second casualty. We went through the method first. Anchor a suitable distance from the shore, checking that the anchor had a good bite on the lake bottom. Then slowly ease out more line and approach the casualty stern first. Transfer the occupants to the rescue boat and if reasonably safe to do so, attach a tow line. Pulling on the anchor line to ease the boat far enough out to restart the engine and the rescue is complete.

In our case, our casualty boat was drifting much too quickly onto the shore, to prevent damage, the rescue crew managed to take hold of the painter (short line attached to front of boats) and while still in water deep enough to use their outboard, powered us away from the shore. The weight of our boat and the thinness of the painter creating a lot of strain on bare hands. You can see from the photo, she did it and did it well. Nothing was lost, nothing at all. Had it been a working job and not a training exercise there is no doubt the newspapers would have carried that image. An image that speaks of determination to do well, to save, to win.

Boat station crews on a training course beach their boats to tip out the excess water. The floating pontoon jetty was too dangerous for a safe landing.
A great day for learning.
Worthwhile and satisfying training that fire crews always enjoyed

The tidal Nene at Wisbech.
The local station's twin engine dory.
(It all began with an ex-police boat from a
disbanded police diving team)

Alongside a moving ship the water forms a hollow into which a smaller vessel can slip . . or surf.
In the same way as it is possible for a following RIB to surf down the engine wash towards the propeller of another RIB. Boating can be most interesting.

These sluice gates controlling the upper river level, were automatic. They could open with no warning. Above, you can see a drum trapped in the eddies, as would be a person. Escape is difficult, death likely.

I negotiated an arrangement with the old National Rivers Authority to utilise the sluices for man overboard exercises, amongst other things.

Fellow instructor, enjoying a high-speed turn.
The boat seemingly creates a 'hole in the water',
into which you can look

Station personnel training on the tidal River Nene.
The ebb tide ran as fast as this type of boat could go.

Tractor and boat trailer recovery in action at Grafham.

The 5 metre Narwal RIB with 40 HP Evinrude

Both images taken at Grafham Water Centre
about 1994
So many stories to tell but no space.

Quickest way to drain a boat on land – tip it out!

All gear secured. Though it did happen once, when the anchor was dropped, and we watched as the unsecured end sunk into the depths along with it! Costly lesson.

Women joined the service

The job seemed to be the domain of mostly white blokes, often those from minority groups not fancying the nature of the work in any great numbers. Then, women turned up. There was much trepidation as stereotypical judgements rushed to the fore. They'll be too emotional, not strong enough, different, need separate accommodation and facilities, cause infatuated firemen to fall out, get pregnant, find favouritism, spoil all the jokes and frequent foul language.

And more. The domain was under threat. Some of these things did come to pass. A retained woman firefighter failed the carry-down test, just not strong enough to keep the dummy on her shoulders and walk down the ladder at the same time. The 'rescued' dummy was dropped from a height. You want the truth? If it had been a bloke he would have been yelled at, told to buck his ideas up and do it again, properly, or he was no use to us. She was led away crying to sit down in the office by a junior officer comfortingly having an arm around her shoulder. How would she cope with wearing breathing apparatus? Was this a sign of things to come? Not really, there were some really great firefighters from the fair sex, as they once called it, though there is bound to be someone who will be offended by that expression. (Being offended is a national pastime now – and a good earner at times). We are a society of offended people these days. The physical tests to qualify for recruitment were much harder than in earlier years and some of the new women were stronger than some of the older men. They brought a different quality to the job, often excellent at road traffic incidents. They brought a greater compassion and empathy, which for the casualties could easily be a life saver.

Some married within the fire service, had children then returned to duty. Good people, good firefighters, good to know and not forgotten.

There was one underlying potential problem with women of childbearing age, (steady, don't rush to judgement!) the fire service had what is known as an 'establishment figure'. Example, say, 400 strong. If you lose any temporarily, for any reason, you cannot recruit more to take their place, and those that remain have to struggle with the loss. You can't pop down the job centre and recruit some out of work firefighters either. Training takes a minimum of three months away from county at an approved training centre.

As it happens, the problem has never arisen, perhaps never will.

**

**Meeting the home
office minister**   -   and   -   **meeting the end** –
organising my last fire exercise for the retained
(part time firefighters) in the smoke house. A selfie
as they call them these days. Training centre staff
wore red caps and lanyards to set them apart from
operational crews. Either the mark of the elite or
the idiot, dependant on what job you had.

**

Everybody out! (Story)

*Location – A disused military base,somewhere in the
United States possibly in the mid nineteen sixties.*

'So, it wouldn't matter if we set fire to it as well
then?'
'No Robert, the entire range of single-story
buildings need demolishing anyway. It's a derelict,
and the military want it cleared by next year. Like

you suggest, it would make an ideal venue for a firefighting exercise. Then simply leave it to burn afterwards. That'll greatly reduce our clearance costs.' Daniel Holland, the local airfield commandant, slapped the palm of his hand conclusively on his desk and smiled across at the elderly but highly enthusiastic fire fighter before him. 'I'll arrange for you to have security clearance to inspect the building. Come up with a plan and a date and let me know. I'll even ask what's left of the airfield crew if they'd care to join you.'

The building was ideal for training, real training, none of that namby-pamby synthetic smoke. The genuine article, something the fire crews could truly learn from and probably talk about for the rest of their lives.

As the kindly, Robert Nelson thoughtfully surveyed the mostly timber structure, he took notes of the two mezzanine floors and the maze of corridors with side rooms of different sizes. Perfect! Many windows were boarded up, making the rooms dark. Even better! There were four or five access doors from the airfield side but all those near the perimeter fence appeared to have been nailed shut, probably to deter squatters. Robert marked on his plans where he would place the fire cribs and considered that he might light them sequentially to create a developing fire situation. That would make the attending crews think ... and work.

Preparations went well, and on the day, Robert had three pumping companies, two ladder units and a heavy rescue vehicle lined up at the airfield entrance. To maximise the benefits to service personnel, several extra crew members from the stations had made their way by private cars. The command post was to be with the newly appointed local captain at his own vehicle, where he would be overseen by an area chief, only there as an observer.

This was a big day for Robert, if anything, the crowning glory of all his years in the fire service. He lit the first crib and waited. Oh, so slowly to begin with, the paper and wooden pallets began to take hold, then faster and faster. Fire can accelerate at an amazing speed and easily catch people unawares . . . and it often did. As the flames began to lick the ceiling and the smoke drop down the walls to partly hide the doors, Robert stepped out, picked his way down the corridor, and made the first radio call from his car. Now it was all up to them. As the sound of engines and sirens broke the airfield silence, Robert returned to light more cribs. The great plan was afoot.

On arrival, the captain allocated two entry points one each for a pump crew and kept the third back for water supplies. Crews from the ladder units were also set to work on running hose and securing water to the firefighting pumps. Four men, all wearing compressed air breathing apparatus, would be sent into each of the two selected entry points, two at the front to locate the fires and extinguish them, backed up by the two others who worked separately to help lift the heavy charged hose around corners and deeper into the building. It wasn't long before the first fire was located, found more by feeling the heat than seeing, they hit the base of the fire with the jet and immediately felt a hot blanket of steam push through their clothing to their skin. 'Down, down,' the branch man screamed. They both hit the floor and thanked god the steam did not follow them. Lying low, with hot gases escaping over their heads, they hit the fire again. 'Something's not right . . . the fire should be out, it's only a crib with pallets.'

Second mistake . . . the building was now on fire; the ceiling had been breached and fire was rapidly spreading unseen throughout the roof void.

Heavy smoke was now pouring out of the eaves and soffits at the front of the building. Clearly now, the roof needed ventilating before a flashover could occur. The delayed ladder crews were quickly withdrawn from water duties and instructed to axe-cut holes in the roof to release smoke and heat. Water supplies were already a serious problem, while airfield requirements had eased, the mains pressure had been reduced or at some hydrants been disconnected all together. Everybody was working like the devil. . . they had friends inside that inferno. Lives were at risk now, and it was a game no longer.

Inside the building, conditions were deteriorating fast, the first crew we followed in our story, were now cut off by the fire, which had dropped down with a collapsed ceiling into their escape corridor, the hose was burned through, cutting off their own supply and reducing pressure to the other crew of four. The second crew heard the stifled shouts for help and two of them left their hose to go and assist. The two remaining were then forced by surrounding flames to abandon their hose and follow it to their exit point, where they joined the chaos outside, as men ran hither and thither, fetching and carrying, calling for help. The six left inside were breathing heavily and keeping low, their air would not last for ever and worse still they could see flecks of flame appearing in the black smoke that rolled along the corridor ceiling towards them. 'This way.' 'No, this way.' 'The back exits are locked, this way to the front.' So came their muffled shouts as the roar of the fire conspired to deafen them.

Confusion reigned, with no hose to follow to safety, they argued angrily with each other at a junction in the main corridor. It was essential they escaped now or for sure they would die a horrible death in there. Panic set in and, despite their training, they split up, four went one way and two another.

Outside, the area chief was as shocked as anyone else at the speed and severity of the fire. He had taken over command and called for assistance and ambulances as a matter of urgency. They were joined by three military officers who had knowledge of the building layout. They began to send small teams in with hoses, just inside the doorways to try and preserve a rescue path for their colleagues inside. They could only hope, lack of breathing apparatus sets and fire severity had robbed them of all chance of a rescue party.

At last, at the far end of the building two weary but thankful firefighters burst out into the daylight, immediately pulling off their face masks and gulping down cool fresh air. Having had only a brief respite they walked amongst the spaghetti of hoses and running men, to the command post. There they hoped to meet up with their colleagues. They were nowhere to be seen.

The building was becoming an inferno, hot gases ready to explode into flame, the ladder crews had been forced to abandon the roof as being far too dangerous, parts of it in imminent collapse. Through the holes they had made, smoke and flame vented under great pressure, the rising plume of black smoke clearly visible for miles.

He had seen enough, 'Everybody out!' screamed the commander, 'everybody out!'

Spurred on by the evacuation signal of deafening whistle blasts, crews withdrew from the doorways and were quickly beaten away from the building by the intensity. Radiated heat was igniting anything in its reach, even exposed hair on the firefighter's heads. Suddenly, one by one, the lost hose crew appeared, stumbling and crouched as if drunk, trying to move away from the middle doorway as a burning ceiling fell and followed them outside. Immediately half a dozen brave souls ran forward, shielding their heads with their arms, to grab their colleagues and half drag them to safety. Once on the sheltered side of one of the pumping engines, they sat down and removed their face masks, the air in their cylinders almost down to the last gasp.

The fireground commander was relieved beyond belief but now must mitigate any more damage. 'Appliances and crews to be moved to safety and a roll call carried out. Nothing we can do here anymore, let the blasted place burn.'

Sometime later, 'Roll call carried out sir, all personnel accounted for, and all equipment made up ... apart from what we lost inside sir.'
'Yes, yes, well done, it could have been a lot worse. We have all learned a valuable lesson today. I can see we must change our procedures; we must know who is in and who is out. We cannot let this happen ever again. Oh, by the way, tell me, whose car is that, still left over there by the perimeter fence?'
'Oh, that's our old station Captain, Robert Nelson's motor, sir. It was already there when we first arrived.'

Did you forget him, like they did? Easily done without plans and rules. Based on a true and tragic event. Firefighters in breathing apparatus now have to leave a name tally with a supervising firefighter outside the building and who monitors their time inside.

**

Smoke eaters

We attended an old wartime Nissen hut at a disused war time airfield, to a fire in stored furniture. With the fire extinguished but the building still heavily smoke logged, my sub officer decided that a bit of the old fashioned 'smoke eating' would benefit this new recruit. So, just like the old days, I followed him into the choking darkness. We hadn't been in there too long before we heard and felt an almighty crump. It was easy to leave the building now as the door was no longer there, it lay on the ground along with the entire end brickwork. Had it fell inside, you might not be lucky enough to read this book! (Careful!)

later, the Sub O was to take another probationer in for smoke eating practise at a different fire. It didn't work out quite so well, with both going to hospital and the new chap staying in for three days. No wonder it was such a dangerous job in the early years and no doubt why the average lifespan of a fireman was less than sixty years.

Modern materials increased the dangers from smoke. Seventeen of the people who died at the Kings Cross fire, died of cyanide poisoning. Cyanide? Off the polyurethane paints and varnish! That's right, the same paint as in your own home.

Even skip fires in the street had to be treated with more respect. Who knows what stuff was in there, cylinders, pesticides, paint, plastics, anything? Shed fires were no longer simple wooden structures. A changing world.

**

210

Sympathy, the old fire brigade way.

The empty factory fire in the photo below was interesting. We could see the smoke in the sky from miles away as we drove towards it. Water supplies were difficult as I recall, with the first hydrant unusable. I was inside with Paul, crouching at the head of the wide wooden stairs looking into what people like to call an inferno. The water dropping down on us from our own jet hitting the ceiling was hot to the touch. Terrible crashing noises came from what seemed to be the floor above. Everywhere internally was made of wood. It sounded like heavy machinery falling through the floor but might have been roof tiles. After a while we were relieved, and on exiting the building Paul became aware of pain on the side of his head. The leading fireman said, 'yes, I saw a lick of flame touch him.' His ear was burned. He sat quietly on the fire appliance waiting for an ambulance. He was in his own world of relative peace with his lot until Roger came by and said, 'bloody hell, you should see your ear!'

That's the sort of sympathy that cheers the heart eh? He suddenly didn't feel as good!

The observant among you will notice
the hose and hose ramps.
The nearest hydrant, almost certainly closer to the
building, was not available.

**

Me on the ladder, my good friend and mentor
Eddie in the window.
A house fire in the drought year of 1976.
The neighbouring county was so busy at the time that
we had to attend to their fire call.
A costly delayed response.

213

It's what we did

While most lay safe and all abed,
we went out, in engines red.
While they, in land of dreams, no care,
we fought the fires, in choking air.

While they could eat their pie and mash,
no time for that, had we,
the dead need pulling from some crash.
Cos it's our job, you see.

As years of life approach December,
long past, we risked our all,
but dreams still come, as we remember,
every bloody call.

**

Twenty years on and hardly a single night will
pass without some memory, often waking to re-
evaluate decisions made, on how could I have
done better.
So many times, in a dream, I hear myself say, 'I
don't have to be here, I could retire you know.'

**

Fire magazine and explosion in Renfrew.

I used to buy 'Fire', an international magazine as I recall. It was filled with really useful articles and reports that never made it into general knowledge within the brigade. They discussed a report on a fire in 1979 with explosions injuring thirteen people and involving stored sodium chlorate. (You can't buy it anymore as it can be used for improvised explosives. It remains one of the best weedkillers ever though.) The report had expressed surprise at the ferocity of the fire, but it just seemed obvious to me, so I wrote to them. I was very disappointed not to see any mention of my expert analysis of $NaClO_3$ when involved in fire. As the months went by, I presumed it not worthy, and yet I'd been looking forward to seeing my name in print. Then in March of 1982 it appeared. Big bold letters and nearly a whole page.
HSE REPLIES TO QUESTIONS
ABOUT SODIUM CHLORATE.
I was mentioned several times as various parts of my letter were confirmed by the HSE. I still have a copy of it, but something has changed . . . I can't understand a word of it anymore.

Below, please find a few excerpts, I've left most of it out, you don't need to know . . . probably.

Failure of the drum would then result in rapid and perhaps explosive conversion of the solid to gas, says Mr. Small, because it cannot exist as a solid at that high temperature and low pressure.

Well-recognized

Mr. Small's letter and queries were passed on by FIRE to the Health and Safety Executive, where great interest was shown in his thoughts concerning the explosive decomposition of sodium chlorate, and a reply given by Dr. W. L. Murray, Deputy Director, Explosion and Flame Laboratory. In his reply, Dr. Murray states:

The two dangers mentioned by Mr. Small—the release of large quantities of oxygen and the possibility of an explosive rate of decomposition—are well-recognized. The release of oxygen could certainly increase the

In his letter, he points out that sodium chlorate ($NaClO_3$) decomposes to give sodium chloride and oxygen. It melts around 256°C and decomposes around 350°C at normal atmospheric pressure. Though stated as pure, the sodium chlorate involved in the Renfrewshire incident would have been contaminated by the pyrolisis products of the plastic bag lining the steel drum container, which was sealed by a steel lid and locking rings, says Mr. Small.

On spontaneous decomposition the reaction would have been rapid enough to be thermally self-supporting, and the decomposition temperature itself might also have been reduced by certain catalysts, eg metal oxides.

Mr. Small goes on to point out that from $NaClO_3$, using the atomic weights of the constituent elements, the proportion of oxygen

**

Who or what saved them?

This is a true tale told me by a fellow fireman of a real incident he attended. We'll call him Bill, for that indeed was his name. He was a highly experienced and worthy fire-fighter who had transferred from another, busier brigade. In his time, he had experienced some real tragedies, of the worst kind, however, this was not one of them.

I paraphrase Bill's words.

'It was an old, fairly large building, plenty of timber in its construction and it was used as a Spiritualist Church. Probably three fire appliances in attendance, perhaps more. The fire was intense and severe, my colleague and I, wearing breathing apparatus and carrying a branch and hose, made our way along a ground floor corridor to tackle the fire. There were a number of doors along the corridor leading to individual meeting rooms, the smoke was thick, hot, and the flames were licking along the ceiling. As we quenched the flames we began to turn our attention to the doors off the corridor, there was one door we could not open, try as we might, even if it was locked we should have been able to break it in. It was impossible, believe me, we tried.

Later on, when the fire was burned out or extinguished, we went back into the building to inspect it. We came to the door we could not open, tried the handle and it opened with ease . . . but we had to step back sharply, for beyond the doorway was no floor – it had burned away. Had we opened it during the height of the fire it is

217

almost certain we would have fell into a deep and burning pit to our deaths.

We will never know what held that door shut that fateful night, but we will always wonder. And be grateful.'

Thanks for the story Bill.

**

The Railway Carriage.

Many years ago, my brigade took part in a multi-agency exercise to test themselves for a major incident. It involved railway carriages on disused track. The railway carriages were on loan from the train company.

It was in error, that they set,
the carriage, well alight.
It burned so fierce, to their regret,
those officers so bright.

When we turned up, to put it out,
they, nowhere could be seen.
While borrowed carriage burned to nowt,
hid in their tents, they'd been.

'Not the smartest move', you'd say,
I wouldn't disagree.
Such skill is why they had high pay,
and ordered you and me.

Thanks to Nick of green watch for photo.

**

He who wouldn't take the monkey home.

This is the cautionary, allegedly true story about immense personal success gained through conscious and intentional neglect of someone else's needs.

Names changed to protect. . . er. . . me mostly !

We'll call him Brutus Maximus for the sake of argument. His subordinate will be played by me. We both worked in the same fictitious training department for a local authority fire service, a hierarchical organisation which requires employees to follow orders and observe the chain of command, regardless of circumstance. Even word, act or demeanour could constitute punishable offences.

Long before I was enlightened about the 'no monkey' policy which Brutus had implemented, starting outside his office door, I witnessed one or two other self-interested behaviours, or so I thought. For example, the department had a limited number of drill books for students and reference. On special days when practical examinations were held for promotion exams each examining officer was given one to use (the applicants were expected to possess detailed knowledge without the aid of such book – in order to rise to the level where they too could forget the contents.) My job was to issue these few books and ensure their safe return for others to use. Brutus lost his, and when I explained he had already been issued with one, he leapt about screaming, 'get me another one then.' Orders is orders as they say, and he duly had his second book.

Prior to an unexpected (by the rest of us anyway) promotion to head of department, Brutus would always join in a practical day out exercise with officer students. It involved a pleasant day's walk in the countryside watching other people struggle with initiative tasks and always culminated in beer and sandwiches on a small remote riverbank. Once Brutus was head of department, he could no longer avail himself of such pleasures and to make sure nobody else did, he scrapped that particular exercise from the course.

One of the tests for recruits into the service was a dexterity test. On this occasion, it was a hacksaw which had been dismantled and had to be reassembled by the student in a given and reasonable time . . . preferably without breaking or losing any bits. For some reason, known only to him, Brutus (with power of life or death over any application) was prepared to pass a particular applicant on a hacksaw that had been reconstructed (you might prefer the description completely redesigned) with the blade back to front and upside down and the locator bolt protruding dangerously from the wrong side. Brutus must have sensed our collective horror associated with employing someone with such dubious skills in an essentially practical lifesaving job and changed his mind. Perhaps the chap was a relative, or perhaps Brutus was just feeling peculiarly benevolent, perhaps somewhere along the line a monkey was waiting.

One more example before I explain about the monkey reference. I was tasked with writing behavioural objectives for the service training programme (incidentally, never implemented despite a year's work, although the local station crews were pleased to have copies). Sometimes he incorrectly would 'correct' the objectives in red pen. When I could see that Brutus was misguided, I simply had the original retyped and submitted. How odd that it received approval next time. Was wielding the red pen just an illustration of power without logic? The behavioural objectives always started off with something like –'At the end of this session the student should be able to do this or that'. Brutus thought this was wrong and ordered me to change 'should' to 'will'. I tried to explain that there is no guarantee that a student *will* succeed only that given favourable opportunity they *should* succeed. Brutus told me quite clearly, 'you *should* write *will*.' I said 'exactly', rested my case and we wrote *'should,'* with his reluctant approval.

Okay, monkeys. Many a time I would visit the office, which Brutus commanded in omnipotent solitude, with some problem that the department was experiencing. For example, 'The breathing apparatus course at the weekend doesn't have enough staff for safety.' Foolishly expecting him to look at the staff rota and transfer someone to assist. His answer, 'I'll leave it with you, do what you can, perhaps someone on the station can help.'

Such answers were never very helpful and often stressful; we were burdened with great responsibility and yet had no power to carry it out. Brutus had the power but constantly declined the responsibility. Remember, we could not complain, for the highly disciplined chain of command leads through the problem himself.

Then one day he confided, in fact he lent me his copy of the article to read, all about avoiding problems – for you anyway. I've no idea what idiot (I'm not afraid) wrote it. The methodology was to see all problems as monkeys. When approached by a member of staff bringing a problem, visualise it as a monkey. Under no circumstances let the staff member leave your office without taking the monkey away with them. If you get stuck with the monkey you have to take it home at night, feed it the next morning and drive it back to work where it will sit on your desk all day annoying you before you drive it home for dinner. There was no sign on the door that said, 'No problems – no monkeys past this point.' It was a secret which eventually led him to two more prestigious promotions culminating in an office at headquarters where his 'no problem' approach must have engendered an ignorant admiration of him. I went there once, after he'd denied ever receiving important documents sent six months previous – his desk was empty, polished shiny and empty . . . all the monkeys living somewhere else I guess – or retired on ill health.

Conscious and selective negligence can lead to great rewards for those who neither give nor take a monkey's . . .

It was never my way, I had enough monkeys to fill a zoo, and I've just released one into the wild. If you find it, do make sure it's okay, won't you?

Believing in monkeys or not, is no protection when you walk into a room protected by a CO_2 installation that has activated. Two steps in and our man was down and out. Invisible gas, huge visible signs on door. None of these things ever stand in the way of promotion though. Or the sale of sour grapes.

My desk during the time I worked for Operations Support Group, mainly writing brigade orders and associated information. Every scrap of paper could be a life saver. No exaggeration.
Mistakes and confusion cost lives.

'One of the greatest tragedies that can befall an officer is to be given the responsibility and denied the power to resolve it.'
But sadly, that's what our management did best!

**

Abseil challenge

The old fire service manuals, first printed long before health and safety laws, outlined a method for lowering oneself by line. We call it abseiling. (rappelling) It wasn't something we ever trained in as it was deemed unnecessary. However, one enterprising chap on another watch had been talking about it and it seems was derided by the others. 'Can't be done. Must be mad,' etc. So, he decided to prove his point by lowering himself from the drill tower using the prescribed method.

At the time of writing this, I just looked at an old practical firemanship manual and sure enough there are a couple of methods shown for lowering oneself using a line. However, I suspect he would have used a variant of these. A search of the internet will tell you that, though it is possible, it is not recommended for safety reasons. Two other points are made. One, it is extremely uncomfortable. Two, it gives painful friction burns. From some height up the tower, our friend began to discover the truth of the previous enlightenment, by the time he reached the first-floor level his hands were so burningly painful that he was forced to let go and fell the rest of the way. I'd say, he proved his point, in a life-or-death situation he could have made it to safety. However, his watch comrades only saw it as proof they were right and no doubt their laughter could be heard across the city.

Right or wrong, I admire his determination to explore and experience what was at one time an approved method of self-rescue.

Of course, today, he would be sacked. Progress.

**

'It is not because things are difficult
that we do not dare.
It is because we do not dare that they are difficult.'

Death – a new reality

On one set of nights at Cambridge, we had ten dead in three separate incidents. One car carrying two youngish couples struck the side of a lorry as it crossed their path. In those days, lights were only front and back, so the sides were hidden in the night. The couples had left their children at home, while they were out celebrating the start of a round-the-world trip. We never followed up on the aftermath of incidents, it wasn't our job. Ours was simply the next incident. It is hard, if not impossible, to lose the images that seem burned into our memories. There are plenty of jobs that see their fair share of the dead. Undertakers for one.

On shift with us was a recruit, who for some reason was allowed to come with us but not do anything. Must have been some sort of experiment. He was ex-military so perhaps he wasn't fazed by his first trips out being full of dead people. It wasn't always like that; he was just unlucky. But not as unlucky as the victims. We had a lot of ex-militaries join us; they were a good bunch with useful knowledge of their own to bring and share with us.

**

London's Burning. TV series

The production company used local firefighters wherever they filmed, that way realistic events would take place without the need for training actors.

I did two sessions as an extra, one a train crash and the other a factory explosion. It was a good earner and they fed us too. The railway one was an all-nighter. One of the tasks was to remove debris from a carriage. It was only a background shot, nothing special. It was real debris though and heavy stuff. What was annoying was when the director shouted 'cut' and 'we'll do that again.' After repeating the debris removal ... and replacement .... three times it was wearing a bit thin.

At the daytime factory explosion, I noticed my boss (an assistant divisional officer from training centre) at the head of a ladder, he was holding a hose and branch and had taken a leg lock. (You put one leg between the rounds (rungs) and hook your foot back through). Anyway, he'd got it wrong.

I shouted up to him, 'you have the wrong leg lock sir.'

Being an officer, he knew better, 'nobody will notice!'

I pointed out that every fireman in the country, when they watched this episode, would shout, 'look, he's got that wrong.' As I walked away, I noticed him change legs.

The TV people always knew where to find the extras,
hanging about by the fancy cakes table.
I guess that's why they had one.

**

'Greengates' – a fire and a life – so what?

Story about an ordinary man in extraordinary
circumstances, his feelings and his actions at a
potentially dangerous fire.

He was a far younger man than now, as he stood
on the night-time gravel road by the big red
engine. It was a remote place far from the lights of
the City, but it had its own light, as a fierce fire
swept through the workshops and cars of
'Greengates' scrap yard.

The gates themselves were indeed green, big solid gates, higher than most men could ever see over. They were locked fast against intruders, of any description, good or bad. The younger man was fully conscious of his thoughts that reflected on life and death. At this time in his life, neither of them had any importance, neither life nor death mattered.

Up and over the gates, strong arms first pulling and then pushing his body over to the other side. Heavy boots dropped into the fire lit compound, it was only then he thought, 'guard dogs,' but thankfully none appeared. Soon hose and branch were passed over from the men on the outside, and one other joined him, Paul, a good colleague. With a shout for 'water on,' they advanced the heavy hose across the compound, hitting the fire where experience had taught them had the best effect.

The all-devouring fire roared and crackled; bright flames lit up the poisoning black smoke pouring into the winter night sky. Closer still they went, closer still to slay their enemy dead. In amongst the glowing workshop fire, pressure was building in gas cylinders; he was aware of the dangers of such, knowing on occasion bursting like bombs, throwing flame and hot metal in all directions.

Still alone, and closer still, they went; then a heavy loud 'crump' and the ground burst instantly into light all around. The younger man crouched lower still, not daring to look up to see what might be coming down. Life or death mattered not, but pain was a different beast; he could still feel that. Burns were a horror they respected and avoided at all costs. Would this demon fire fall, like the angel of death, from the heavens and engulf this crouching figure in the yard?

He waited; it was to be life, and life with no pain; after the fright, it was their turn and onwards they pressed, now supported by more colleagues, and after many labours and many hours, the demon was finally slain, though it had taken much with it while it lived.

Still, to him, this younger man than now, life nor death mattered naught, but survival with honour would do him for a while.

Author 1984, about the time of Greengates Fire.
Story was written then.

**

230

Probationers – games and initiations

Poor old probationers, often victims to pranks by their new colleagues. In some ways it was a psychological test, to see the reaction and how they might evaluate their new addition. Were they up to the task? Whatever it was? Probably highly illegal now and a sacking offence – but I would put it to you – it did have merits!

I'll just share a few I heard of.

The new recruit would be challenged to beat the old hand at holding their breath. 'Easy,' would think the youngster, eying some knackered old chap near retirement age. Game on. Two sinks would be filled with water and the person who could hold their head under the longest would be proclaimed champion. What a great way for the youngster to prove himself. Heads in the water. As soon as the young chap's head was in, the old fellow took his out. As the young chap came up, gasping for breath, the old fellow ducked his head back under. The youngster then waited about a minute in astonishment before the old fellow had to surface. They would never let on.

Railway horns at 3 miles

After parade, the first thing firefighters do is check their kit and the equipment for readiness. We carried a small trumpet like railway horn for use at track side incidents. Some poor chap was persuaded that he should climb the drill tower and sound the horn in the direction of the nearest fire

231

station and listen for the reply while they tested theirs. I'm not sure how many times they sent him up. Cruel isn't it?

I'll briefly share a few other 'games'.

The boat race. A tray of water is set up on a low table, competitors knelt at either end. The objective was to blow a floating matchstick to the far side. They were encouraged to practise, and with lots of cheering on, they enjoyed the fun. Then it was time for the serious part, the big race. A test of prowess and honour, to become a champion, lauded by their peers. Ready, steady, and they crouched close to the tray, GO! Everyone who was in the know, dodged out of the way as the referee slapped his hand hard into the water, drenching the unhappy victim's close by face. There were those who didn't quite take it in the spirit it was meant!

The aircraft raid.

I witnessed an epic at an end of course do at Moreton. Worth trying to picture it. I have no idea how the victim knew nothing while everyone else seemed to know their part. Anyone with a leather or sheepskin jacket was chosen as pilot. The chairs were laid out in the shape of an aircraft with engines on each side, pilot, navigator, mid and rear gunners. The engines had to rotate an arm like propellers. Three people hummed the dam buster's theme throughout the entire performance and an orator gave a running commentary as the bomber took off and flew to Germany. There was conversation between the crew, not the engines obviously, 'Pilot to navigator, over' etc. This was magnificent theatre, very entertaining. They dropped their bombs and made for home but were hit by anti-aircraft fire, conveniently acted by yet another would-be thespian. The humming continues. 'Navigator to pilot, rear gunner has copped it over.' The rear gunner slumped over his seat. 'Mid gunner to pilot, starboard engine smoking skipper.' The pilot feathers and shuts down the starboard engine. It's not looking good; they are on reduced power as they fly low over the Dutch coast making for blighty. The dam buster's theme is in full flow. The port engine is getting tired but encouraged by all around to keep going. Then tragedy strikes, 'Navigator to pilot, port engine on fire.' At which point half a dozen blokes pour beer over the poor chap. He had an aching arm and his clothes soaked in beer, but an incredible spectacle, worthy of the finest acting troupe, but these were just a few blokes having a night out.

Battle of the spoons.
I'd seen this a few times but by far the best was with a chap from Nottingham, robin hood country, and who had made the grievous mistake of criticising the course during a debrief. Tonight, they took revenge. Two chairs are placed back-to-back with a reasonable space between them. The contestants are each given a dessert spoon which they place in their mouth. They take it in turns to stand behind each other and strike the other on the top of their head as hard as they can. Our pal from Nottingham made another mistake, he played to

the crowd when it was his go, and to a rousing chorus of 'Robin Hood' he did his best to crush his opponent's skull with his spoon. You might well know that no power can be generated by this method, but it certainly can, if a third party smacks them on the head with a hefty ladle. Our man from Nottingham winces with pain and stands, imploring the frenzied crowd to sing more of 'Robin Hood', he then theatrically opens his arms to bid us quiet while he exacts justice on the guy he thinks has hurt him so much. Fortunately, it didn't go on for too long as he would have been a candidate for concussion the way the ladle holder was laying into him. Justice was served. God bless Robin Hood.

Ah, those were the days, and they won't ever come back. Glad I was there and lived through them.

**

Peterborough Cathedral

The funeral

Colleague killed at fire

I was working at the training centre that day. Suddenly an inexplicable sense of doom filled the place. Something had happened somewhere, and it must have been truly terrible. Anyone who knew, was saying nothing, but the tension was palpable. It was only later in the day we were to discover a number of our colleagues had been involved in a large explosion and that one was dead. It was the 22nd of March 1989. Some twenty miles away at Fengate, Peterborough, a lorry carrying 780 kg of high explosives had detonated. In the blast, 107 people were injured. I'll leave you to imagine the difficulties faced by firefighters caught up on the first attendance. After the explosion there was nothing left of the vehicle itself.

John Humphries was stationed at Stanground where he had worked with blue watch for a number of years. Along with hundreds of others I attended his funeral at Peterborough cathedral. His coffin was transported on the deck of the turntable ladder and carried in slow march between rows of uniformed firefighters that stretched from the main road all the way to the great cathedral doors. Representatives came from all over the country. There was standing room only inside the packed cathedral. There were lasting pains for those involved in the incident. Pains that last a lifetime, no matter how long or short that is to be.

**

235

ISO 9000 and Investors in people

Does everybody operate like this? Or was it just our lot?

ISO 9000 was (and perhaps is) a quality management system. My boss and I were sent to a neighbouring county where the course and implementation package were to be presented. We sat in the classroom and my boss thought he'd better put them in the picture, 'we are only here to observe, our brigade hasn't signed up to it.'

'Ah, there's a surprise, for you. They have signed up and you are their representative.' My boss turned to me and said, 'I'll do it and you assist me.' In his car on the way back to county, he said, obviously having had a change of heart, 'you do it and I'll assist you.'

I won't go into it too much as it would require a new book, but it transpired that I was to do it and he was to oppose it. What a turnaround eh? The thing the bosses didn't like was being accountable, putting their name to something that could go wrong. Example, non-compliance form. We had rules and if they were to be broken, whoever was in charge had to explain why they were ignoring the rules and put their name to it. You can guess can't you, not very popular. So, if we needed four people for a ladder drill but we only had three, what were we to do? The boss had no intention of finding more staff or indeed any intention of writing his name on any instruction. Usually they just said, 'do your best, see what you can do.' Not their fault if it went wrong was it? I mean, they were at home when it happened.

On the advice of the brigade's psychiatric consultant, I later moved departments to be free of . . . . well, just be free I suppose. My ideas were too often suppressed by incompetent superiors. (There's a good word for you.) We could, with little extra effort have become a certified training centre for power boating and sold our services to other brigades, but we didn't.

Another officer took over the job of processing ISO 9000 to fruition. He worked on it for a further six months before it was finally kicked into the long grass. We can't have senior people made accountable. Whatever next. Where would it end?

While trying to maintain instructors on undermanned weekend courses I accrued seventy-eight hours of overtime at the training centre, and which could only

be taken back as time for time. It wasn't transferable to the following year so the officer in charge selected some more dates to clear the debt.
This time represents at least four occasions where I worked all week plus the weekend, only to start over again on Monday morning. My boss was at home.

You have no doubt heard of Investors in People. I was sent on a one-day introductory course. I found it invigorating on one hand as I saw all the benefits the system offered a developing workforce and I also found it disheartening because I could see it would never work for us. We didn't invest in our people. There were, however, a few very useful ideas that we could safely adopt, and which would bring us benefit. There was no way that we would ever be hanging an 'investors in people' plaque over our front doors. Having been sent to find out and having written a suitable report on what could reasonably be achieved, I never even had a reply from headquarters.

Investing in people . . . what a joke.

**

'Destiny comes not through chance but by choice.

You are your own destiny.'

**

238

New year and doing an exchange shift

It was new year's eve and I had agreed to work a
night shift for a sub officer who wanted the night
off. He paid me a sum for doing it and was very
pleased that he could then spend the evening with
a new love in his life. I didn't realise that the
brigade would be paying me too, and generously
so with nine hours double pay from midnight. An
added bonus for a man who lived alone and had
neither new nor old love of his life. Sometimes life
is like that. The station was having a disco and
party night for paying guests and the duty crew
looked after them. Just before midnight I had a call
from fire control. A fireman had gone down with
food poisoning and the hospital had asked for
confirmation on what he had eaten at a fire, earlier
in the evening. Would I check the dustbins at
station and locate the 'hotcan' in question for
evidence (some strange food in a self-heating tin –
I never ate one, so cannot say what they were like).
As I rummaged through the bins at the back of the
station to the rousing strains of Auld Lang Syne, I
considered my lot. It was less embarrassing at the
bins than at the party. Duty calling was a saviour
at times. As it turned out, the food had been okay,
it was some chicken he'd eaten earlier. Scare over.

**

Life jackets? ... and we called it training !

It was a serious business, indeed, a matter of life and death, we had to trust never to let each other down. . . at least not to knowingly let each other down anyway.

We were in at the deep end in more ways than one. We were keen, disciplined and enthusiastic but the almost non-existent training and insight we had been given was a pauper's substitute for a properly developed experiential apprenticeship whereby we could have learned from those who were truly skilled and from other's mistakes.

We were going to have to make some of our own. . . and we did that too.

Firstly, we had to find somewhere suitable to carry out our training. When I tell you, it was all to do with life jackets you'll think, 'Aha – they'll need water. Mmm, a swimming pool will do or perhaps a river.' Good, I like your thinking, however for health and safety reasons we must discount the river, or indeed the fine outdoor pool that had been unused over winter – we couldn't be allowed to use it in case the water was dirty – even if it was perfect for our needs.

'Well, you've got lots of swimming pools around, just use one of those,' I hear you suggest.

Excellent idea; and mine too; somewhere clean, with showers, changing facilities, local, secure parking and lockers etc., in fact, ideal. Now try finding one that will let you even look at their pool in full fire kit, (operational firefighting clothing including boots and other carried equipment), and that's if they have a vacant slot in their swimming programme, usually completely filled by schools or the public.

With a great deal of hard work, gentle persuasion and compromise we found a place that would help us. We were allowed two fenced off lanes and must ensure that all our gear was thoroughly clean before entering the pool area.

Sorted! All gear to go in the station's big washing machine and allocated solely to the 'life jacket course', which in itself was only a couple of hours long. Life jacket training was to be done whenever the pool was available, even if it occurred weeks prior to the rescue boat course itself.

We had two types of life jacket, one was a bulky full-size unit, and the other was a lightweight slim waist jacket type that had to be inflated manually by pulling an activation toggle. Well, that little red toggle wasn't always easy to find in good conditions, so I reasoned that in full panic mode it would be nigh on impossible, hence I always chose to wear the ready to use with no thought version. The red toggle was to have other implications too.

Though we covered some theory poolside it was essentially a practical course. Despite having a warm water pool to use we had to pretend otherwise for our 'cold water entry' drill. The intention was to clamp the mouth and nose shut on entering the 'cold' water which hopefully stops you breathing in the river when your body is shocked to gasp for more air; a natural reflex as you'll all know from your own cold-water experiences. Before jumping in the water be sure that the strap on your fire helmet is undone. . . if not, your neck will be, as your body sinks lifeless to the bottom leaving your head floating attached to your fire helmet.

Okay, so now we are safely in the water. Test one; can we actually get out again on our own. Test two; can we rescue a colleague. . . just to tow them a short way to the bank and assistance. . . some of which may later prove dubiously useful.

There were different ways in which this assistance could be manifested and big Dave, otherwise known as 'Rab', was to demonstrate one method, how to lift me out of the water assisted by the water itself. Easy; take one good strong grip on the life jacket 'handle' and proceed to bounce the floating casualty in the water, pushing them down and pulling up assisted by the lift of the water. Up and down we went, or was it down and up? Then, when the momentum is right, haul them up and on to the bank, or in this case poolside.

'Rab' was a big fellow, ex Royal Navy diver, which is why we'd seconded him to our group; down I went and up I came, then down I went again and up again, at which I began to wonder just how many times I was to be 'baptised', then down and only partially up as the strap on the life jacket slipped undone and the hole through which I had put my head earlier shot upwards sounding like jet aircraft engines on afterburners as it passed by my ears, taking a shade of skin with it

242

and leaving friction burns behind. My ears cooled mercifully as I sank into the pool and 'Rab' stood with the students on the poolside holding up high in one hand the 'rescued' casualty, one empty life jacket.

Yes, you are right. . . they couldn't stop laughing.

Some mistakes were obvious to avoid. . . sometimes only in retrospect mind you, for example, Fire Fighters might have to wear breathing apparatus as well as life jackets; which one do you put on first; The heavy cylinder of breathing apparatus or the light waist coat type life jacket? Answer is Breathing Apparatus; if you do it the other way around the life jacket cannot usefully inflate but might try and squeeze the life out of you!

Now back to those waist coat type life jackets. . . inflated by a small carbon dioxide cylinder activated by a trigger attached to the infamous red toggle. Normally the writer writes history in their own favour, leaving out their own foolishness and mistakes, we shall deviate from that norm here and write a confession. (It's not all my fault mind you as we really should have been trained better ourselves, we were victims of constant appalling management. . . there, I feel a little exonerated and able to continue now.)

We were teaching something of which we knew little ourselves; well, arming the gas cartridge wasn't just a simple matter of screwing in a new cylinder, oh no, the trigger had to be reset first. If you didn't reset the trigger you could pull

243

the toggle until the cows come home and the jacket will never inflate.

I know this from first-hand experience as I did it to myself – no wonder I never liked that type of life jacket. Thinking about it now, I see it as a design fault; it should have been designed such that a full cartridge and an armed trigger were a prerequisite for the toggle to indicate it was ready for use, and not how it was. . . either badly connected or already a discharged cylinder. Another quick tip while on the subject. . . if a carbon dioxide charged life jacket needed topping up through the wearer's manual inflation tube you'd better make sure you never breathed in !! Instant unconsciousness would be the result, possibly followed by some other catastrophe of which you would remain blissfully unaware. It was a life jacket type I always avoided, though it remained a favourite with the operational fire crews.

What is even worse, I'm ashamed to admit, is I set up a life jacket incorrectly for someone else. Apologies, Nicky. She donned fire kit, breathing apparatus and 'serviced' life jacket, then in she went with a splash at the deep end of the pool. We could see her under the clear water, (I suppose better than dirty river water in the light of this last revelation, eh?) struggling to find that essential and elusive red toggle, all is okay, we, the watching students and 'instructors', see her struggle and her success. . . she finds the toggle and pulls, the look of relief on her face is short lived and turns to puzzlement beyond the clear plastic face mask of the breathing apparatus. Puzzlement turns to exertion and desire. . . to get out of the water. . . and, as she struggled to the pool edge, students looked on with shock and I with a touch of guilt and knowing. Another mistake under the belt, all in the name of training.

We made light of the situation, I mean we wouldn't have let her drown would we, . . . and soon the next student was preparing for the ordeal by mistakes, er, I mean by training.

**

'The greatest hazard in life is to risk nothing.
By not risking you are chained by your certitudes, and
are slaves, having forfeited your freedom.
Only one who risks is free.'
Zen Osho

**

"Only as high as I reach can I grow, only as far as I
seek can I go, only as deep as I look can I see,
only as much as I dream can I be." –
Karen Ravn

**

'Whatever your practice,
over time, you become.'

**

Tales from the Smoke House – a BAI's story.

From basic training with pumps and ladders, the fireman would move on to more advanced training in the use of Breathing Apparatus (BA); he would learn and practice search and rescue techniques, care and maintenance of equipment, procedures about entry control, firefighting, emergencies and teamwork. It's not just teamwork, but individual skill, knowledge and intuition, that makes a good BA wearer, for once the team is inside the incident they are on their own; often blinded by smoke and darkness as they peer through their misted-up visor. Cut off by toxic smoke and dangerous conditions from the rest of the crew and officers – whatever the BA team face inside the building, they face it alone, in the dark in more ways than one, in a strange place.

The Fireman must not only know how to find his way back to safety but be able to conduct 'entrapped procedures' should his route be barred by fire or collapse. Horror stories of fire-fighter's deaths in the most panic stricken and desperate of ends should be enough to focus the BA wearer's mind on his means of escape. When air runs out in the cylinder, desperate men have torn off their masks, breaking the neoprene straps, only to succumb to the choking hot gases that envelop them; fingernails torn from clawing hands as they tried to escape rooms that were not their way out – though they thought they were. Orders given to flood underground bunkers to extinguish a fire, knowing that the BA men sent in earlier must be dead already, their air run out long before – surely enough to focus the BA wearer's mind.

The BA wearer must know all the secrets of doors and their mechanisms, what height the handles – and how many too. Sliding doors and recessed handles, doors that swing closed behind them with no handles on the inside, and doors that open from upper floors straight to the long drop and the street below. A never-ending catalogue of pitfalls and traps must be learned – glass doors, mirrors, electricity, moving machinery, gas cylinders, gas leaks, fat fryers, pet pythons and on and on .... As the BA wearer progresses in experience he nurtures his desire to teach others of his learning.

In the old days the heavy compressed air cylinder was made of thick steel, the face mask had an inner mask that pinched the wearer's nose uncomfortably throughout the wear ..... No chance to scratch an itch .... And woe betide the wearer that inadvertently sneezed. A length of strong personal line was attached to the set harness, his pressure gauge allowed him to assess 'time' past and 'time' left, also attached at chest height was the distress signal unit –The wearer pressed a button and a high-pitched buzzer sounded, (useless in high expansion foam) The early ones sometimes only worked if you gave them a good whack – it didn't stop them being issued. They could only be turned off by the key held outside the building by entry control in fresh air. The torch was a low output affair as used down coal mines – it's hard to know how miners could see anything with them either ! – usually made of copper and on a simple hook this lamp would hang on the chest strap of the BA set …….. that is until it slipped off – a frequent occurrence.

The Breathing Apparatus Instructor (BAI) had to know all this and more, he also had to know how to set up and monitor exercises efficiently and safely, how to instruct and guide the student BA wearer and mentor the more experienced wearers and those Officers who came once a year for their refresher training.

Ah! The Officer's refreshers – those Officers who professed to know so much, so important, changed people's lives with Masonic promotion opportunities, earned lots and did less. The BA refresher – a chance to see that they did some real work – on occasions it wasn't unknown for extra fuel to go on a hotter fire to settle old scores.

It is, I suppose, to be expected that they would make mistakes, but, consider this, that at fires or chemical incidents they would be responsible for the direction and safety of BA crews. So, was it really so important that they put their BA sets on upside down, tied themselves up in their own lines, or separated from the rest of the crew? …. You make your choice!

For the operational BA wearer all these could prove fatal errors – and these Officers were their leaders.

It was up to the BAI to put all this right.

In 'tales from the smoke house', the smoke house is a term given to a room or building in which heat and smoke are produced either artificially or with real fires.

All new retained fire-fighters always attended a BA initial course with qualified training staff consisting of a Station Officer and two or three Junior Officers. Someone amongst the staff had to be a BAI, if not all of them. I recall one such course when our Station Officer was not a BAI, but being the senior rank he was in charge, and what he said, went. It was going to be a week like no other. We only had three of our own retained fire-fighters to train but two firemen from the nearby USAF military base were to join us.

It was evident from the beginning that our Station Officer was going to show these 'colonials' just what 'real' firemen were made of. On day one, under 'easy' conditions, just to acclimatise wearers to sets and procedures, I had one wearer try to pull his mask off. I did all I could, without physically restraining him, to stop him and calm the panic. To remove the mask other than outside with the Entry Control Officer is a cardinal sin, especially in panic – what if he did this on a real working job – how many of us would die trying to save him – never mind his own life.

Well, it was to no avail, he tore off his face mask, then realised the enormity of his actions. As he calmed down, his sorrow was evident. The matter was discussed with the Station Officer, and it was decided that, as we were short on numbers and the Fireman realised the error of his ways, that he could stay on the course .... until two days later that is!

He resigned and left on Wednesday lunchtime, at the same time as one of the USAF firemen, who'd been sick in his facemask while in strenuous heat and smoke conditions at one of our smoke houses – again a serious matter and potentially fatal. The exhalation valve is designed for the passage of air, not stomach contents, and the small ori-nasal inner mask is also where your fresh air comes in – so you end up breathing in your own vomit – yup – not nice and when you are in a toxic atmosphere, to remove your mask, is no better an option is it?

So, we are now down by two, and by the end of the afternoon we were three down with the remaining USAF fireman succumbing to the rigours of the underground tunnel crawl – a gruelling simulated sewer exercise rescuing a full size, 12 stone, dummy – (only one exceptionally talented team in all the exercises I took part in ever succeeded in making the whole distance, usually teams would only make halfway).

Now we only had two students – but this was still ok, as they worked in a pair while one of us did the Entry Control job outside. Next day, Thursday it was, our leader had gone ahead to set up the smoke house at a village station. Inside there were many obstacles - an old factory roller conveyer, furniture, partitions, a set of stairs, and crawl areas as well as a small fire. The crawl areas were 45-gallon drums with the ends cut off so that the BA set on the Fireman's back ensured that he would have to lie prone in order to squeeze through. As you went forward, reaching with your arms, it wasn't unusual for the sleeves of your fire tunic to ride up, exposing your arm – now, coupled with the fact that the Station Officer had placed one of the big fan-driven industrial paraffin heaters butting up to one of these drums so it was glowing red hot, it wasn't surprising that one of our chaps got burnt. Now we're down to one!

I drove our injured chap to the hospital for treatment – he was okay and well enough to attend the last day. As BAI's, I don't think we would have lost any students, as our point to prove was not to impress but to teach …. But we were not in charge.

I was a BAI working at the training centre attached to a small central fire station, which, in the early days had a small brick shed fire house. It had a small but tortuous two-level labyrinth of wooden 'tunnels' with some very constricted and awkward turns – if someone was ever trapped in there for real it would have been extremely difficult to get them out due to the restricted access. Our best hope for an emergency procedure was to open the two external doors and extinguish the fire, so getting fresh air inside to the casualty.

We would take it in turns to be the BAI safety observer, (on the inside), or the safety officer outside that kept an eye on things externally, watching the entry time clock, the temperature and listening for distress signals.

I recall once laying on the hot wooden boards of the upper level, the heat from the boards was already paining my legs. As I lay there in that braising carcinogenic concoction of hot gases, I knew it would be impossible for me to go any higher and over the partition wall to drop down to the ground floor near the fire. It can be only 50 degrees C near the floor but as much as 500 degrees at the ceiling – I'm sure you can work out the consequences yourself as we roast meat in the oven at only 200 degrees.

So, there I am, laying there, the observer and 'rescue' man, waiting for the door to open and the BA crews to enter for their training. The door did open – but it was Dave, an old-fashioned BAI, – only opening the door so he could throw some more fuel on the fire! So, you see, the BAI was in the thick of it much longer than the crews, we were first in and always last out.

During one of the exercises in that little fire house we nearly 'lost' an officer, and a senior one at that. (We have met him a number of times in this book already.) It was a guideline exercise, the crew of two would carry a big bag of special 'string', one end of which was tied securely to the outside of the building in fresh air; they could always then retrace their steps to safety. Come to think of it, it was a very silly place to do such an exercise – it was equipment more suited to big spaces – still, we just followed orders.

The Officers were nearly out; they were just negotiating one of the tightest corners in the lower 'tomb' level when the lead officer became entangled in the guideline, unable to free himself due to the restricted space, nor could his colleague help for the same reason. The small, lightless, smoke-filled fire house is little more than a gas chamber; their only hope is the cool air they breathe from the cylinders on their backs.

A distress signal sounded; the Station Officer in charge, shouting, 'Get the doors open!' By doing so we could get fresh air and light inside. From where our Station Officer crouched in the open doorway, hot smoke billowing out above his head, he could see the trapped man, who was trying to pull his face mask off. Our Station Officer screamed at him, 'keep your mask on; keep your mask on!'

All to no avail; the mask was off, but luckily by then cool fresh air was filling the lower ground of the fire house.

The reason for the panic?

He had no air left. At the training centre we were experiencing problems with this particular type of breathing apparatus. (Ego and a sense of justice permit me to tell you it was me that discovered and reported the fault – though we continued to use those sets for some time before the problem was resolved. Of course, those with power and high office weren't those who ever had to wear these sets – perhaps then it would have been fixed earlier … or is that too cynical?).

When the wearer breathes, reduced pressure in the mask triggers a flow of air until the pressure rises again and turns it off … until the next breath. The process is quite noisy and in order to listen to others it was necessary to hold your breath. The fault in our sets was that occasionally at very low pressures when you were at your most vulnerable, tired and short of air, the air supply would trip into a constant flow, wasting your air and gushing it out of the exhalation valve, your ten-minute safety margin reduced to two or less – and nothing you could do about it – please spare a moment to consider this.

Probably the fact that we nearly killed one of our senior officers focussed the mind of those responsible for our safety, and who previously had deaf ears to the fault.

Before I was a BAI, and before the health and safety executive had too strong a strangle hold on the fire brigade, we could light fires and use them for realistic practical training. I was involved in one such exercise that spelled the death knell for live fires at our main station's smoke house.

Cambridge station smoke house in the background.
The control panel and air vent to the left.

It was a building of two floors with an internal concrete stairway against the back wall; there were large semi-permanent vertical partitions within the building to make life more complicated and challenging and a huge heavy fire basket sat in the middle of the ground floor.

The Watch (a group of Fire-fighters that always worked together on shift) was split into two, one half to wear BA and do the training and the other half to do all the organising outside. Then, at a later date we were to change roles, ….. we never were to have our 'revenge'.

Our task was to collect 20 kilo drums from the upper level of the windowless, blacked out building, and deposit them on the ground floor. We were all in pairs and connected by a short personal line (4 feet) to our partner.

Well, it was going okay, we made a couple of trips up the stairs and down with our loads. It was becoming rather hot in there though, as flames from the fire rose to the ceiling and hurried across to the stairs where they met us on our way down. I called a halt to any more crews going back up. The fire was accelerating in intensity – thanks to a big chap called Andy who kept throwing sheets of hardboard on before going back outside and closing the doors.

From our position we could see the flames now crossing the ceiling and entering the stairway about halfway up. We still had one pair of wearers upstairs; then they appeared; the lead man, taking the steps in haste and two at a time – not bad in boots, fire kit and BA, dragged behind him, staggering like a puppet, on the end of the personal line, his colleague – a lighter and less fit man than he it must be said – how he made his feet land on steps we'll never know.

We were all down and relatively safe, and we exited through the emergency doors into the fresh cool air and reported to the watching Officer – but he had already seen the state of the fire through the open door and ordered the exercise aborted and the fire extinguished.

The last man down? Much to the amusement of all, his hair was singed all down one side, changing the shape of some sort of curly wig type 'perm' he'd had done the day before – that too had amused us. We couldn't wait for the 'return match', and then we'd show 'em what a real fire was all about – it was never to be, live fires were discontinued at our station from that day. ….. Damn!

What happens next is a real must …… for the training centre was to have a new, state of the art, thoroughly researched and innovative architect designed operational training building, which was to be constructed in place of the small brick, labyrinth gas chamber we mentioned earlier.

During its construction, someone, and still anonymous, but probably off of the operational fire station and not training centre, had been nosing about in the building at night. They were fairly certain someone had been in there as they found the hardened footprints in their concrete the next day.

This brought about a massive overkill response – one that any sane person would look back on with regret – 'Anyone caught entering the smoke house will be put on disciplinary proceedings.'
Fair enough I suppose, they were in charge, but how useful it would have been for all concerned if those who were actually going to use the building could be aware of what was going on – and dare I say it, contribute? It might have stopped them building a multi pitch roof, (excellent and just what we did want), clad with highly brittle concrete roof tiles which cracked or broke when we put any weight on them, (not at all what we wanted). We could no longer use the roof for any training, if we did, the roof would soon be bald.

After the building was opened with due pomp and ceremony and the Chief Fire Officer posing for the press, we began to use it. Things soon started to go wrong. The fire room, (lined with special ceramic tiles – that just happened to be carcinogenic – still, not to worry, that also went for most of the dust and fire bi-products that layered the inside of the building) had a big insulated heavy metal door to the outside and two similar doors on the inside, above which were transom openings, which slid on rollers so that we could open or close the amount of heat, fire and good old sparks entering the training area. Well, these didn't last five minutes; they failed on their first use, also to evacuate the smoke in an emergency, powerful fans were fitted in the drill tower and a great, two floor height, louvered metal shutter fitted to allow the fresh air in. This they did rather efficiently – 'good thing', I hear you say, except that they too failed – in the open position, negating the value of a once dark and hot smoky smoke house which became light and full of fresh air.

You might think that we, the real and only users of the building might become a little frustrated by then – and you would be right.

Still, all was not lost, someone had a brilliant belated idea – (and was probably promoted instantly) – why not get the users and the designers together, let them sit round the table and sort it out. *(Because we can't.)*

I was present at the meeting. The architects had designed a fire room in which we could light large fires to heat the building; they were quite shocked when we told them that the temperature at the head of stairs was as high as 160 degrees C and the fire room was achieving temperatures of about 400 degrees Centigrade. 'Oh dear,' they said, 'We didn't know it would get that hot ...... the solenoids we used are only good for about 80 degrees.' Well, that explains why they didn't last too long eh?

'What about fitting better solenoids?' we offered.

'Not possible,' they replied, 'they don't make any that cope with that heat.'

So now we have a complex design built around solenoids you can't buy; do you think early consultation might have averted this? So, do I.

So, here we have a state of the art, architect designed operational training building that is no longer operational. We had things sorted in the end, resorting to simple manually rigged and operated systems that did the job – sort of.

If only they had let the BAIs in at the beginning.

The new building had a control room with a great electronic 'dashboard', most of which we never used. There was a monitor through which infra-red camera images could be relayed and recorded – very rarely done as the connectors for the camera inside the building didn't like the dust, heat, smoke and humidity either. We could play sound effects throughout various areas of the building of our choice – trouble is they didn't supply us with any. The tape we used was a multiple recording of a small extract from a forensic fire reconstruction video; it had a realistic fire and suitable noises to accompany. During the filming of the test the scientists were caught out by the speed and ferocity of a quickly developing and intense fire, they had to evacuate the area in a hurry with someone bellowing, 'everybody out! Everybody out!' This shout was also on the recording we were using. I remember once we had just sent a crew in rigged in BA to affect a search and rescue operation in heat and smoke, we were playing the tape to create a more realistic scenario, but it was not long before the crews burst out the emergency exits.

'What the devil are you doing out here, where's the casualty?' a BAI demanded.
'We heard a voice saying everybody out!' their muffled voices shouting through their masks.
The BAI, in his most pleasant and diplomatic manner, in a soft and friendly voice explained,
'Yes you did! .... But that's NOT for YOU; you're the fire brigade – back in and be smart about it!'

There were manholes in the floors, with 4-foot drops, shielded by heavy metal covers which we could remove for different exercises, like simulating basements or sewers etc. Even though instructors were totally familiar with the layout of the building, (perhaps there's a clue there), at least two fell down them; I know of at least five people that suffered the same fate.
Instructors on occasions faced more immediate life-threatening experiences.

The fire room had a big metal brazier, the thick metal bars of which were sagging and distorted from the intense heat generated in there. There were no visible door handles on the inside, the only light, the light from the fire. The fire would be stacked with paper, kindling and heavy wooden pallets, and then lit by the BAI some thirty minutes before the visiting fire crews arrived for BA training. With the fire burning well, it would be topped up with more pallets, each being carried through the doorway and thrown in, sending a shower of sparks into the air, the BAI shielding his face as best he could from the radiating heat; the heavy metal and insulated self-closing door propped open against closure.

That heavy metal door was to almost take the lives of two BAIs on separate occasions. The events were officially kept secret by the first victim, though privately shared between us fellow BAIs; I'll share just one with you.

It was a winter dark evening time, and the BAI was there early and alone. He entered the fire room and lit the fire; breathing apparatus was never used in these circumstances for practical and procedural reasons.

The flame started to rise and take hold; the fire had a firm grip on the timbers by the time our BAI – a big man – heard the unmistakable loud metallic thud and clang of that great metal door slamming shut and, outside, the locking mechanism snapping into place. For him it was too late to dismantle the fire of fuel, serious burns would be inevitable, he rushed to the door and searched for a handle – if there ever was one under the insulation and thick wire mesh that held it in place we never found it – anyway it's an irrelevance – he was not going to find it, not that night! He needed to get out of that fire room, and damn quickly, no good waiting for the arrival of the fire crews, they wouldn't think of looking in there, literally the last place they would look, by then he would be long dead; having died the most terrifying and slow death by the radiated heat; in the morning it might be that just a few bones and buttons would tell the tale.

Well, fear and an overwhelming desire to get the hell out was coursing through his very being.

There was a way out!

It was through the same hole that those soon to be searing hot flames would be leaving and then it would be impossible – one breath of those hot gases and the lungs would be irretrievably and fatally damaged. He had to act quickly; how he managed to pull himself up to the height of those transom openings above the inner doors even he will not know, how he managed to squeeze his huge frame through that small opening he will never know, and how he managed in the darkness to find the floor some eight feet down and headfirst he will not know. What he does know is that he is out – alive – safe.

What he achieved would surely be impossible if it were not for those terrifying circumstances in which he had found himself.

Some of what we did, what we saw, taught, discovered and learned is always with us in our minds. We had to know more, experience more and stay longer than those we taught. We strived to help improve their chances of survival when wearing BA out there in the world of less predictable fires, that didn't have sprinklers and controlled ventilation systems and where life was truly threatened.

I hope I've given you a taste of some of the honest and sometimes truly frightening tales from the smoke house.

Forever strangers – forever comrades.
Breathing apparatus course at the
Fire service Technical College

19/1/91	30 mins	BA D INSTRUCTION	HEAT / ... MARCH SMOKE HOUSE	INS 1
12/2/91	30 mins	BA D INSTRUCTION	MARCH SMOKE HOUSE HEAT / SMOKE.	TC 10
3/2/91	30 min	BA D INSTRUCTION	BOI Smoke House HEAT / SMOKE	TC 10
4/2/91	45 mins	D	March Smoke House Heat / Smoke BA. INS.	INS .1
12/3	25 min	D	M Heat / Smoke	M234
14/3	25 min	D	O Heat / Smoke	M234
8/3	25 min	D	R Heat / Smoke	M190
20/3	20 min	D	T Heat / Humidity	M 234
27/3	30 min	D	O Heat / Smoke / coms.	M 231
11/4	40 mins	D	BOI Smoke House IND BA. SMOKE / HEAT	TC 1
16/4	30 mins	D	March Smoke House	INS 2
16/4	30 min	D	March Smoke House	INS 2
17/4	80 min	D	BOI . Smoke house .	INS 2
13/6/91	30 mins	D	BOI Smoke house Schemes Industrial	INS 2
15/10/91	45 mins	D	Derby Smoke House instructor demo Heat/smoke	2/3.
16/	~	—	C.A. House BOI	INS 2

Between November 1990 and October 1991, I donned breathing apparatus, mostly in heat and smoke, thirty-seven times. A sample is shown above and includes a course at Moreton in the Marsh.

**

Flashover training

Whereas we taught the principles and procedures for it, we didn't have the facilities to engage in practical flashover training, so we had to send people to another county where they had purpose-built units and specialist staff. Even for long serving firefighters it was still something special to experience. They used modified metal container units in which they lit a decent sized fire and controlled the air flow. Once inside, we witnessed the hot gases ignite at ceiling level and observed the reaction to introduced water spray. There was one marked demonstration of too much water. The water turned to steam, and we could feel the heat immediately penetrate our clothing. The trick was to cool the unburnt gasses enough, without creating enough steam to make us a 'boil in the bag' thing. It was run by good people with whom we enjoyed the training and the comradeship.

**

Dave's piano gift.
You'll not really understand this photo, for the same reason we cannot listen to music through someone else's ears.

The place is the operational fire training building, including furniture and an old piano donated by a good colleague, Dave. Dave is no longer with us, nor has been for many years now but his memory lives on.

The time, one winter's evening. I am alone in the darkened concrete structure; the big fire crib of wooden pallets is ready to light. This is my last time in this building in which I had worked for many years training firefighters in the use of breathing apparatus.

As I typed the above, for some unknown reason the smoke detector in my house went off, I stopped typing to go and check. . . there was no reason for the alarm, which sounded only briefly. . . and has never done this before nor since. Perhaps it was Dave's spirit just letting me know he's still about, or perhaps someone else, just letting me know that there is still some connection. Most odd. My fears are allayed by thinking so.

As I waited alone, I wandered the building, checking that all was safe and ready for the visiting retained fire crews that would be training that evening. I lifted the lid of the piano that by now had seen much better days, and I played a few notes. I had more skill in moving pianos than playing them though, I must say. I'd set the camera up on timer so couldn't make a nice pose, however, it is a reminder of the passing of many things, life, time, friendships, duty, and sadness too.

Music for my ears only, just as it will always be so.

267

You will have your own occasions in life,
don't miss them.

**

The lone night shift

Frowned upon back then and probably illegal now, I once did a fifteen-hour night shift on my own. Once the day shift signed off, I set about my duties. Every appliance and vehicle had to be inspected and checked for fuel and defects, all equipment accounted for, and each breathing apparatus set checked for minimum stored pressure, all torches checked for battery strength. Station van, Land Rover, Hydraulic platform, water tender, and water tender ladder were completed after a couple of hours, delayed by a metal bucket jammed inside a side locker so that I couldn't open it. No use if we had a fire call – had to be cleared. During the evening I heard the relays clicking on the VFA communication system to control. They shouldn't have been operating if no one was using the phone. So, who was on the station making the call? No one!

I called fire control and asked them about it. They suggested I tried the office across the yard in case it was off the hook there. It wasn't and nobody was about. All in darkness. In the end it was sorted, I can't remember how, but I do remember what it felt like to do the night shift on my own. And we had a fire call during it too!

**

The station cleaner

Good chap, hard worker, his Sicilian heritage might have given him a slight temper. Witness several knuckle marks in the plastered walls. We got on fine with him, but he had a dislike of the officers, especially the station commander. One day, while the cleaner was on holiday, someone emptied the cleaning cupboard and shifted everything to a much less convenient place. They then converted the original cupboard to a photography dark room and changed the locks. You might imagine the enraged reaction when our cleaner discovered the plot on his return from holiday. (Perhaps a mafia gathering? Only joking!) He was livid and in loud half Italian said, 'I kill him.' Well, you could have sold tickets to watch this event, as we didn't care much for the station commander either. As it happened good sense prevailed. But he didn't forget!

I struggled to fully understand him when he spoke. On one occasion, after some garbled preamble, I thought I'd respond to what he said with a short laugh. His face changed to that of the judge reaching for the black cap. There was no joke. He had apparently told me that despite great sacrifices and all he had ever done for his son, who now was a motor mechanic, his son wouldn't help him fix his car. And I'd laughed at it! Lucky for me the station loudspeakers called me to the sub's office. Phew.

**

The Victorian Fireman's Axe. (Story)

These events are shared from the perspective of the axe itself, for who are we to say that the inanimate has no right to share its story?

We were such good comrades, that old fellow and me; constant and dependable companions; we'd been together for over thirty years; faced death and disaster many a time, side by side; the crumbling stairs, the choking acrid fumes; just a way of life for us both.

I suppose, in a way, we were both forged in fire. He was born around 1874 and I in 1892. We worked together in a small but industrious little estuary town. The tidal river ebbed and flowed carrying various cargoes for warehouses not so far from our station. Often, the firemen would pick up a few 'silver darlings' for dinner from the herring fishers on the quay.

Though it wasn't a big station it saw many changes, even whilst I was there. The horses and steamer were still there when I started, the place was heated by a coal fired boiler and there were various outbuildings storing hay and the like – I never went in there myself, had no need of me I suppose – but others told me how it was.

Though the place was somewhat spartan, it was clean. Twice daily the tile-red painted floor was washed and was clean enough to eat off; the brass work of doorbell, steps, fire door mechanisms and all the equipment was so polished you could see to shave in – not that they did – many of the men had fine sets of whiskers. A row of polished brass helmets rested on hooks above smart, collarless double-breasted tunics – the sort of tunic that inspired every man to stand tall and proud that ever felt its fit. It was with this tunic I would wait, waiting for the bells to go down and my comrade to come and fetch me.

For a few years, until it died of old age, a scruffy stray dog was adopted by the station. They used to laugh a lot at his antics, but greatly admired the dog's courage so close to fires; I think they called it 'Braidwood', though I cannot tell you why, but it did seem to amuse the firemen considerably. Anyway, that dog lived the life of Riley, well fed, slept by the boiler, and then, when the alarm sounded, would run out into the street, and follow the men to the fire. What a life, what a lucky old thing, ah, how I envied that dog.

Where was I? Ah, yes, change. The station was to have the new electric light, and later, though the large brass hand bell still hung on its bracket, we were to have a big electric bell fitted. Every few years the station would be sent a new pumping appliance, (those on the outside, who I was

271

informed knew nothing, called them fire engines). The old one would be zealously polished and cleaned with pride as it would be sent to a less busy station, and we had a reputation to honour. The new one would take its place and result in a flurry of activity, starting it up, stopping it, starting it up, pumping water, men running with hoses and ladders with lots of shouting going on from the watching silver helmeted officers. My comrade never wanted to be one of them, it just wasn't for him, for he had a deep sense of duty which he felt was only truly satisfied at a place the men called, 'the sharp end'. For this I am eternally grateful as it's the only place I can work. He was good at what he did, come to think of it, so was I, we were a formidable team, us two.

Then, one day, he didn't come in to work; I was placed alongside some boots and on top of some folded uniform and fire tunics, then taken by the Brigade wagon to a place I later learned was called, brigade stores.

After all my valiant and unstinting service, I was to be incarcerated, in a small dark room, in a box.

Occasionally the door would be opened and, along with the store-man's hand, light would come in and bring a glint to polished and waiting steel. The hand would fumble then select from the box, and one of us would be taken. Sometimes the choice was rejected and the 'un-chosen one' was thrown at the back of the tiny wooden room, never to be allowed back with us in the box.

We, who had given so much to change other's destiny, were now uncertain of our own.

Sometimes, when this door was opened, we could see young men in new uniforms, with buttons bright and thick black polished leather belts. One time, when the door was left open in error, we saw one of our brothers, a chosen one, being handed to one of these keen smart young men. He grasped the ash handle and made some amateurish chopping action with the blade. It amused us - he would learn. He was only young and now he had one of us to look after him – to stop him sliding down a roof to his death, to open locks that barred his way, to quick release the pressure in a snaking hose dangerously out of control, oh, so many things our brother would show him. He put the axe in his belt pouch and the cupboard door was closed. We were never to see either of them again. It seemed forever, that we stayed in that small wooden prison.

When all was quiet outside and the store-men home to bed, we would share our stories .... of action, of noble strength and relentless courage; like our comrades, we were prepared to do all that was required and to make sacrifice when duty beckoned. We often wondered why, when we had served so well, and given so much, what we had done to deserve a fate such as this. Strange, but one morning, about lunchtime, we overheard the store men discussing the state of an axe that had been returned much the worse for wear, chipped blade, scorched handle. Finally, we heard, ...'If only they could talk, what stories they could tell us, ... ah, well, ... I'm afraid it's in the bin with you,' and so saying, the store-man dropped our valiant brother into the rubbish.... Too bad the cry for mercy fell on deaf ears.

If only they knew of the stories that were being told, just a few feet away.

I well remember telling my brothers, one cold night, about the last shout I went on with my old comrade …

It was a deadly dark and bitterly cold November night, a winter wind pattered sleet on the dormitory windows, it was the last of our twenty-four-hour duty and tomorrow would be a rest day. Then, in the small hours of the morning, the big six-inch electric bells burst fearsomely into life. Men, driven by duty, habit and a shock of adrenalin leapt up from their beds, blankets cast aside and eyes wide staring open as they rushed for the rest of their firefighting uniform.

They could smell the smoke filling the air as they prepared themselves to turn out, the driver doggedly hand cranking the petrol engine into life. Two more men pulled the thick ropes that unfolded the great red wooden doors of the appliance room and they looked out into the winter street to see, by the light of the engine's lamps, a mixture of driving sleet and billowing, thick, yellowed smoke.

They knew, tonight of all nights, this was a working job they had on their hands.

It wasn't far to go, just down the road at one of the old wharf buildings that backed on to the river.

It was a hotch potch of a building, part stone, part brick, which had been added to many times over the years, making a labyrinth of secret places the devil fire could sneak undetected to trap and cut off the unwary. It was a building of three floors and part basement, about one hundred yards deep and about thirty yards wide. It was used mainly for storage of mixed goods, almost anything could be there, wool, timber, grain, jute, anything; the fire seemed to be located on the second floor and was 'showing a light', flames being visible through breaking windows. The Sub Officer had himself and six men; he sent two of them quickly away to locate and set into a hydrant, the pump man stood by the controls. The Sub Officer pointed and shouted his orders, 'take a line of hose around to the windward side and play the jet through any windows on the second floor …. Break them if you need' ………. and two more men were gone, struggling with their heavy canvas hose into the dark. Now they were three, 'Right,' he said, trying to sound confident but deep down knowing this to be a daunting task, they would need the Angels with them tonight, 'Come with me; we'll have a quick look inside. Bring a couple of lamps; let's go.' So close we were to the fire, and so far we were from help, it would be twenty minutes at least before another crew might arrive, we were on our own.

The main door was padlocked against us, it was a job for me, and I didn't hesitate, with my brave but aging comrade … a tough steel point through the hasp and a wrench of the ash handle and the lock was in two. Just as we took our first wary footsteps through the doorway, one of the men from the hydrant reported in, out of breath, gasping, 'Line

275

in from hydrant, Sub, but jet's hardly reaching second floor!'

The town only had a two-inch diameter water main, and the pressure was never much good at the best of times. There were no ponds and any wells in the vicinity would not last a minute.

The Sub seemed to stare into the air as if looking for an answer, then, realising that something must be done quickly or the fire might spread to other buildings, for sparks and glowing embers were already being carried in the wind, he made his choice, (as we too must make our choice in time), he shouted loud, above the roar of the fire now competing with the roar of the engine running nearby, 'Right! Get the pump moved to a corner in case the building comes down, find anyone in the street that can help and set into open water, get a second jet to work.' As the man turned to leave, the Sub Officer shouted after him, 'and take him with you, get going!' This left just the Sub Officer and us two. I think he kept my comrade with him for a couple of reasons, to save him from all that arduous, heavy work setting into open water with that awful cumbersome rubber and wire suction hose, and secondly because of all the years of experience and knowledge that could prove invaluable inside this growing inferno.

'Come on,' shouted the Sub, 'let's find the stairs.'

It wasn't long before we found them, they were made of stone, not good this, stone stairs had been known to collapse without warning; give us timber stairs any day, you knew where you were with them. The noise increased as we made our way

276

ever upwards, so great was it that we didn't hear the call from below. 'No water!' The tide was out, too much mud.

They fell back to setting into the hydrant, exhausted and covered in cold mud from their exertions to reach the water's edge. They had, however, improved their water supply by shipping another standpipe into a water main a street away.

The crackling jet was now beginning to play through an open window, quickly turning to steam and occasionally hitting a glowing cast iron pillar, one of many that supported the floor above.

Sharp and very hot slates were now cracking and sliding off the roof to the ground below, tiny burnt holes sprung leaks in the canvas hose, the crew with the jet sheltered as best they could. They didn't know what else to do; they could only follow the last order. They waited amongst the falling debris for assistance to arrive or their Sub Officer to return.

'What a God forsaken mess,' cursed the Sub officer, as we surveyed the stacked goods of the first floor. Timbers above creaked and the sound of falling slates and spalling stonework filled our ears, 'If only we could salvage some of this ..... but... just the two of us ....' His voice trailed off, then, 'what the hell was that?' The Sub stared at us disbelievingly. We had heard it too. It was a scream, almost inhuman in nature. 'For God's sake,' the Sub gasped, 'there's someone up there; what the hell are they doing here?'

'Night watchman, that'll be my guess Sub,' said my comrade in a calm but urgent manner, 'it'll be old Fred, he's got a gammy leg .... that's why they gave him this job. .... I'm pretty sure I can find him Sub.'

'Go for it then, take care, you damn well come back safe; I'll check on what's happening outside and get help to you as soon as it's possible,' with that said, the Sub Officer's big, dirty hand patted him admiringly on the shoulder and in an instant he had melted away down the dark stairs to the ground floor.

I had a moment to reflect on this ... what did my comrade mean, '**I'm** pretty sure **I** can find him', what happened to the '**we**', after all we wouldn't have even got this far without my help. Then I realised I'd fallen into the old ego trap, I'd forgotten that what endeared us most to the Brigade was adherence to our motto, '*Service needs no praise,'* it brought us the greatest of respect and

278

status. We asked for nothing but to be allowed to serve, we were almost invincible.

We found the next stairs, now of timber, and had to brave a small fire on our way upwards.

I tell you, I remember thinking, 'I hope he knows what he's doing!'

Frantically, and beginning to choke in that killing air, we searched for old Fred; we found an open window and looked out and down, there in a crumpled heap on the cobbles below, lay the reason for the scream, it was indeed old Fred. Just out from the window to the right was an old cast iron rainwater down-pipe, when young and fit it is easily possible to climb down such as this, if you know how. Perhaps Fred had considered this his only way out; it was a young man's game that, even for us it looked decidedly dangerous, and we'd done it before. We turned to leave but that cursed fire had sprung its trap and spawned destruction and chaos behind us; now it was we that must find another way out.

Water sprayed in through a broken window on the far side. With plaster off the walls in places, timbers creaking and bits of broken slate peppering the floor, we made our way across, at least there some fresh air came in. My dear comrade gulped in some clean air, then he called out to the men below. At first, they could not hear him but then they did, almost everything was dropped as they rushed to retrieve the wooden ladder from a far wall ... we could hear the orders snapping out apace, we knew they would be here soon .... 'Head away ... extend.... well ... lower....

under run …. heel to building …' A panting, red and whiskered face suddenly appeared at the window. …….. 'Bloody bars!' ….. 'Bloody barred windows!' …. 'Give us yer axe 'ere and I'll try and break one free!' I was quickly passed out through the broken glass into the slippery new hands still numb from the soaking cold of holding hose and branch.

I fell. Clonk, clonk, clonk as I hit the rounds of the ladder on the way down, accompanied by an anxious cry of 'stand from under!' I heard the heavy fire boots thumping down the ladder … 'pawls, step out!' screamed the now shocked and solitary fireman footing the ladder, then I was passed from hand to hand, and we returned to the head of the ladder, at first he shouted out to my brave comrade that all would be well, that we were back, and he wasn't alone anymore. Using my chisel shaped spike our whiskered rescuer hacked at the stonework that held the bar in place. There was no voice from inside, there was no sign from inside …. I wondered if he had gone back to try the drainpipe ….. all we could see from outside was the deep red glow of a big fire in a slow rolling sea of choking dark smoke, then it happened …. Whether it was the roof that gave in, or the hot gases had ignited – suddenly all hell broke loose and searing hot gas and flames appeared at every window with a loud but dull 'crump'. The fireman on the ladder was forced to duck down and away from the window to save himself. He climbed quickly down, shouting, 'get some water in through that window – quick – for God's sake ......'

The Sub Officer turned up, extra crews had arrived, water supplies had been improved and progress was being made.

My comrade? I don't know, I heard others talking .... 'He must have found another way out' ....and another say, 'yeah, if anyone could, he could. I wouldn't be surprised to see him come out that front door any minute.'

I didn't hear or see any more as the initial crew were relieved and sent back to station, and I along with them. They made a pot of tea, opened the door of the boiler, and stared silently, with both hands clutched around hot mugs, drying their wet clothes, at a fire that was now not their enemy but their friend. I remember thinking, as we warmed up safe in our station, 'I pray he's alright.'

Dawn was beginning to break, and a new day commence.

Well, you know the rest, I can't imagine anything bad happened to my comrade, if it had, I should have been with him, much guilt remains in my heart that I didn't stay with him, if only I hadn't slipped... but I just can't think that. It's too much to bear.

I've been many places since first being forged in fire and I can still do today what I could do one hundred years ago given the chance. I spent many wasted years lost and alone in various cupboards, but for the last ten I've been an ornament on a shelf in a retired fireman's home – I don't think his wife likes me …. hang on … here she comes with that damned duster and polish …. must stop now got to go … thanks for listening to me, not many give me the chance you know …. if only they would …. that's all we ever needed …. just a chance ……that's all… not much to ask, is it?

**

'There was a time before our time,
It will not come again,
When the best ships still were wooden ships
But the men were iron men.'

R & S Vincent Benet

Station public address system

We had a succession of station officers 'commanding' our watch. Only one of them was excellent in all ways, the others varied in mediocrity. One in particular was a transient nuisance to us. In those days, the night watch would rest overnight and be ready for work at seven in the morning. We had a cup of tea before station routines and then breakfast. Our wayward station officer thought, unnecessarily, that he should remind us of getting up time. We were already at tea when he made an announcement over the address system. One of the watch members answered with a cryptic comment. In reply, our misguided station officer played some music very loudly over the system. 1812 overture or something similar if I recall. Shortly after this, there was a phone call from the police station next door to tell us we had left the yard speakers on. The drill yard speakers were designed to be loud enough to carry over the sound of running engines etc and were normally switched off at night. No doubt the sleepy occupants of nearby silent houses were surprised at this musical wakeup call at seven on a Sunday morning. He was an idiot. Guess what? He too was promoted. How did they do it? No idea.

**

Return to station
After a call out, which you will realise we called 'shouts', any used equipment required checking, cleaning, replacing. Regardless of time of day or

night, the vehicle would be washed if necessary, any blood from accidents cleaned off salvage sheets and then hung up to dry, hose exchanged for clean lengths, same with lines, nothing was ever stored wet to rot. Fuel checked and refilled on the appliance or light portable pumps, wet uniform placed in the drying room, tyre marks mopped in the appliance room and a fire report submitted to fire control. Perhaps a cup of tea and a chat together would finish it off.

The drying room was a place of comfort and nostalgic reminders of past jobs. Always warm, dry and smelling of smoke. Not everybody's choice of perfume! Tunics fresh from various disasters hung in their rows, silent witnesses to an often-untold story.

**

Suicides, disturbed people and the insane.

We had regular shouts to the local mental hospital, often to the drug and alcohol unit but occasionally to a real incident in the main wards. Why would someone set fire to the bed they are in? No idea, but they did. They would also sit on the railway tracks that ran by the rear of the hospital. The staff wore no identifying clothing – you work that one out for yourself and your guess is as good as mine. On arrival we would be met at the main door by a staff member. One occasion, my colleague was greeted with prompt efficiency, 'this way, follow me,' and was led into the catacomb like corridors

284

of the old Victorian building. You've guessed haven't you? It was an inmate. There was a youngish lad who always excitedly greeted the fire crews and pretended to be on to fire control with an imaginary handheld radio. He was always there, always pleased to see us, even thrilled about it. One of the old hands gave him a fire service cap, which thrilled him even more. It, however, didn't thrill the hospital at all as he was in there as a compulsive arsonist.

There was an excellent sub officer on another watch, who went to a suicidal man on the guild hall roof. Our man went up on the turntable ladder to have a chat, this was long before social training and negotiators were thought of, he had a word with the bloke, told him it was dinner time at the station in ten minutes, so he hadn't got time to hang about, and if the bloke wanted to come down with him he'd better make up his mind quick. Our colleague's nature, manner of speaking and presence did the trick. My guess is that not many could pull this off. But he did.

There was a chap in a tree outside one of the colleges, he was surrounded by police, and firemen holding out a stretched salvage sheet to catch him should he fall or jump. (It wouldn't work anyway, have you ever tried catching something large falling from a height?) A leading fireman off our watch, Scotty we called him, was trying to talk him down and had placed the short extension ladder nearby to the 'disturbed one'. 'Don't worry pal, all will be fine, come on down and have a cuppah at the station with us. No one will hurt you,' he promised in a kind and assuring voice. The guy seemed to become agitated and started to climb higher, at which point Scotty used the ladder to bash the bloke's fingers hard, causing him to lose his grip and fall. He fell into the salvage sheet, which predictably immediately hit the ground and just as quickly was filled with very keen and burly policemen who carted him off to the cells. Perhaps he did get a cup of tea after all.

On the edge of our station turnout area there was a home for the criminally insane. Even if the building was on fire, the inmates were not to be released except into a secure compound of relative safety. High fences and razor wire were just part of the structure. Luckily for all concerned it stayed fire free.

The brigade also endured the loss of their own through suicide. For them it must seem like the only way out of some imagined place they are trapped. To the observer, it is inexplicable.

**

We're all searching for something,
it's just that sometimes we don't know what it is.

**

286

Moreton in the marsh.
Fire service technical college.

*Foam prevents any spilled fuel fire breaking out
around them as they advance with spray protection to
find the isolation valve.*

We learned so much. Such as, that you can put an
un-gloved hand into liquid nitrogen and remove it
un-damaged, that fuel tanks when heated in fire
can BLEVE – boiling liquid elevated vapour
explosion – exactly what it says it is. We learned
how ammonia tankers can fail after turning on
their sides, embrittlement fractures occurring from
friction heat then rapid cooling by gassing off of
contents. The end of a tanker was the worst place
to stand, much like the business end of a rocket. We
visited Aldermaston, a top-secret base that anti-
nuclear protestors put on the map in the nineteen
sixties. Even the map on site didn't show the base,
just woods! We also learned other things too, like
in hot sunny weather, the accommodation block

furthest from the water supply didn't get any! We rescued people from the tops of busses, from lifts and from being skewered with a scaffold pole, there wasn't much we didn't have a go at.

It was a home office run establishment and as such potentially subject to attack by terrorists. In consequence we were warned never to leave our bags unattended on site. A further consequence was discovered by the poor chap whose unattended bag was relocated to the old airfield and blown up. One has to smile. It sharpened our minds though.

Even in very hot weather we were expected to wear shirt and tie, and none of the exercises were softened to account for the temperature. While I was there once, a chap was hospitalised with heat stroke.

When I first went there it was still run by the home office, even the catering. However, privatisation being the latest thing since sliced bread, they sold off the kitchens and workforce to a private company, who quickly slashed the wages, rendering some of the work unviable. The home office run kitchens obviously did not wish to spend more money on feeding us than absolutely necessary. In consequence we were condemned to eat our way through old freezer stocks. I have no idea how long the ox tongues had decorated the freezer walls, but they appeared on the menu more than once. I recall a chap I sat next to in the mess hall, finding a large, deep-fried moth in with his chips. They must have run out of ox tongue that day.

Once you had initially booked in at the gate with the security services, on subsequent trips into town, you only needed to hold your keys up at the windscreen for the guards to lift the barrier. It was a fairly lax affair and two blokes once managed to get in by holding up a dead mouse.

Usually, the course members would gel and become a self-supportive unit. On occasion, someone would not quite fit in. There was a chap from Scotland that brought his own TV with him and remained quite insular. During a practical exercise where he was in command of a lift rescue, he did all the work himself, not involving the crew he was intended to direct. It set him apart. One evening, a group from the floor above, dangled a tape cassette player on a length of string outside his window. It was a Max Bygrave's tape and apparently it not being to his liking it annoyed him. With his curtains drawn, and never considering it could be outside his first-floor window, he proceeded to investigate by knocking on all the surrounding doors. Someone suggested it could be from the room above him. The rooms were poorly sound insulated anyway. He stormed up the stairs to confront the inconsiderate music lovers, only to find of course that it wasn't there either. It was hanging right outside his window all the time.

I felt a bit sorry for him at the end of the course too, as some of the blokes had found an old broken TV on the airfield dump. They presented him with it as an end of course award.

You can't be insular in a team game.

Now, talking of games, the powers that be (or were) at Moreton, always pitted any two sister courses against each other. Not only in technical marks but in sports as well. Well, one of the events was a run around the airfield perimeter. I couldn't run for toffee and told them.

They replied, 'No matter, you must compete, or we lose points. Just have a go.'

So, I did. As the gun went for the start, I was soon left behind and by halfway, they had disappeared to the finish line. All but one other struggling runner from the opposite team. What was most disconcerting was the first aid van kept driving slowly by each of us ... no doubt wanting to earn their keep and hoping for a chance to use their skills. They stared intently and prayed but I prayed harder and came in second from last to a rapturous reception. You'd think I'd broken a record.

The concrete ship at Moreton. We trained for all eventualities. In the hope we wouldn't sink one – or die on one. The tunnel escape by the propeller shaft was much cooler than the BBQ like metal stairways above the engine room fires.

**

The Divorced Fireman.

Divorced he was, by many years.
Of course, mistakes he'd made.
She minded not his pain nor tears,
such, dreadful price, he paid.

He pondered on the past gone by,
of things, that could have been.
And dwelt upon the reasons why,
he still remained unseen.

He wondered if she'd fret at all,
when he'd rushed out the door,
to where in danger, he might fall,
and then be seen no more.

He risked his life each time he went,
'gainst frightful terrors dared.
He thought upon his past life spent,
and if, she'd ever, cared.

**

It is tough being demoralised at home, then donning uniform and trying to hide the sadness while being an active and leading member of a close-knit fire crew.

Trying to start a new life post-divorce wasn't easy, it meant starting from scratch obtaining a mortgage and paying for it along with child maintenance. Low paid menial tasks became necessary to pay the bills. The days of phoning the Samaritans may have been over, but the pain of losing my children was severe. I made the mistake of applying for a potentially useful secondment into the fire prevention department. Too late it dawned on me just what I had let myself in for. Permanent days meant I could no longer earn a few pounds extra and on which I depended. One of them being Christmas presents for my children. I explained my predicament and needed to return to shift work on operational duties. They dismissed my pleas. On arrival at the new job, the first thing I asked for was holiday days off. They weren't too happy to discover they had such a reluctant employee and arranged to have me removed as soon as possible.

Pity really, had circumstances and priorities been different it could have proved a valuable career move. We make our own choices though.

**

On call as a station officer.
Not the same as being on call as a firefighter. Back then, at home, I'd sleep with easy to don clothes ready by the bed, socks already prepared at the end

293

of trousers. Speed was essential, no time wasted. Then the run or cycle like crazy to reach the station. During daylight I could arrive before the main station bells stopped ringing. Control didn't need to know where you were, just that you would turn up at the station when called/

Not quite the same when an on-call station officer. (They don't call them that anymore). At all times, you needed to know where you were and indeed, where it was they were sending you. Sounds simple does it? You needed to be consciously aware of almost every road number in the county and where you were upon it. The radio could burst into life at any moment and ask you for your location. While on call from home, your telephone had to be free for incoming calls. You needed to hear, (not so good, as a level of deafness had already paid me a visit), the precise address. Sometimes I would ask them to spell. It was easier. Then in the darkness of my car with frosted windows I had to locate the address on a dimly lit map, unable to clearly read the words. All the time against the clock. You are expected to be on the road and mobile to the incident. Demisting the screen, clearing the frost, all biting savagely into that precious time. I wasn't the sort of officer that sat on the driveway, waiting for the stop message to come in, nor the one that took an hour to reach the incident. (For the sake of a name we'll call him Kevin)

I was tasked to run operational debriefs but after doing only one and writing an over honest report,

I was removed for someone more 'empathetic' to officer's misgivings.

You cannot deal with an incident if you cannot arrive. Obvious. So turn up.

I recall, a chap I worked with was thrilled to receive a call to a village pub fire, (going well it was). He smiled in a happy superior manner as he bid us goodbye. Later that evening I was mobile to a retained station that I supervised and heard lots of officers being called over the radio, 'Your location over?' Each one in turn replied that they were many miles from the village pub fire. Then they asked me.

'Unfortunately, just entering the village now.' The laughter from fire control could be heard as they replied and sent me to the pub. The officer who I replaced was my colleague who had been so keen earlier. However, he was on 'earlies' and should have gone home at 1700 hrs, but he couldn't, he was stuck at the fire, no overtime payments no compensation.... just the way the cookie crumbled. He was very relieved to be replaced and cheerfully sped off home.

When danger came . . .

Not for them to say, 'We're brave',
though risk their lives they would,
when danger came with threat of death,
through hope and hell, they stood.
To a man, the foe they'd fight,
regardless of its form,
and danger comes with threat of death,
in darkness, fire and storm.

I know their thoughts; I feel their pain,
for with them once I stood,
and danger came with threat of death,
but not once cry they would.
When fearful shouts for help came in,
loud bells would raise alarm,
then danger and its threat of death
was met with strength and calm.

The siren wailed, the road it cleared
and urgently they'd drive.
While danger stalks with threat of death.
'Hang on, 'till they arrive.'
That dreadful fire, it seemed to breathe,
and life to terror give,
as danger grew with threat of death,
they must not let it live.

Fire is dead and people saved,
the crew returned to base,
all danger quelled from threat of death,
relief on every face.
No coin they ask, but honour due,
reporters, beg their name,
though danger lurks with threat of death,
none who's there, seek fame.

**

Flood lists for officers

Rather than attempt to send fire crews to every
flooding call, they sent officers with a list of
premises to attend, assess the requirements and act
accordingly. One rainy night, I am given a list. First
call is to a lady who lived alone and had noticed
that the water in her toilet was rising. I explained
that there was little she could do as the sewers
were back filling with flood water, should it

overflow into her house, her best option was towels against the door. But actually, there would be no escape from it. As I left her house, she started to speak to me – mostly about the builders and the guttering. Meanwhile I am being drenched with monsoon like rain, while she stood in her dry comfy doorway. From there I went to an estate where anyone in uniform might be an unwanted police officer. I eventually found some assistance from a man who shouted back into the house, 'it's okay, it's a fireman!' He explained the address I wanted was along an unlit path to the rear of his place. There was no sign of flooding, but I knew I should check. The gate was secured by several entwined bungy straps. I wondered why, until I saw the size of the dog flap in the back door. I left furtively, quietly securing the gate so as not to disturb whatever guard beast they may have that ate people in uniform.

Next was a pub by the river. Evidence of old sandbags that had long since rotted was an indicator that they knew they had a problem and couldn't be bothered to fix it. I couldn't be bothered either. That made two of us, except they could have afforded to protect their property with ease. . . and a few new sandbags. Then on to the next call. By now it was getting quite late, but a list is a list, regardless of what the clock says. It was an old brick-built cottage, a large expensive property alongside a main road. There were no lights on, so I knocked. Eventually a man opened an upstairs window, my guess, he was in his pyjamas, 'What do you want?'

'Fire service, I've come about the flooding call you made.'

In a very annoyed and I'll admit, condescendingly annoying tone, he said, 'that was hours ago, the water's all gone now. Don't you know what time it is?' He didn't add the word 'dopey', but he might as well have. I could see there was no water there, it was obvious. Perhaps he might have thought about cancelling his panicked call for help. Why bother eh? Soon my list was completed, and I could go home, find dry clothes and prepare for the next shout.

**

Crown and coroner's courts.

I've been to both. The coroner takes precedence in power. I was most impressed. I had arrived more than punctually to deliver a statement and a fire report on a fatal incident. The previous case was about to start, and the chief witness was late. He was a surgeon whose patient had died after being sent home. The coroner said, 'you are late, I don't want to have to send you to prison!'

'Yes,' I thought, 'this is the place for justice.'

The case is irrelevant, but I would like to express how genuinely good the coroner was. Brilliant.

Then, it was my turn. This was very difficult for me, as the family of the deceased baby were there in the court. In all probability it was an older child with matches that started the fire. Who wants to know one of their children has killed another through stupidity and disobedience? I was not a trained fire investigator but had dutifully excluded all other possibilities. The coroner made it easy. He stated simply what he considered the facts and that they agreed with the fire report. I didn't have to look at the parents and say, 'your boy killed your baby.' However, I don't doubt they kept their smoking materials in a more inaccessible place thereafter.

Crown court was different, I never even made the witness box. We spent a day in an office with some police officers who told us the prosecutor had never won a single case. I could see what they meant when he interviewed me on the morning of the trial and had me mistaken for someone else. The guy was guilty. Guaranteed. (allegedly) He was drunk, had an argument, set fire to a first-floor room and prevented anyone from leaving the house. His wife called the brigade, pleading for help and reporting her husband as having set a fire. I listened to the tape at fire control. As we arrived in the court car park on the second day, we noticed the defendant driving out. The case was over. It was over the day before, but the prosecutor could earn another day's pay if he strung it out to the next morning. Apparently, the defendant's wife had asserted that her husband was too drunk to climb the stairs, and by default he couldn't have possibly set fire to the bedroom. Once her evidence was accepted, the case was over. Is there something obvious here that you can see but the court could not? Staggering incompetence in our judicial system. Was there no evidence the wife was perjuring herself? What about the tape with her screaming? 'Help, help, my husband has set fire to the house!' Oh, well, that's life eh?

Let's hope that prosecutor was never promoted to judge. Any bets?

**

Reflections on society.

We saw the whole range of human activity or depravity, from the kind old lady who made a cup of tea to malicious calls and the thug in the street who wanted to show us his knife. There was the child who burned the bed to stop the abuse, the children's bedroom with chicken wire nailed over the windows, the brim-full urine bucket at the head of the stairs - too full to move, and the dog owners that lived with dog crap all over their living room. Then there was the rich guy with the tiger skin rug in his salubrious accommodation at St John's College. And in between, everything you could possibly imagine. People in general have little time to tidy up before the fire brigade arrives! I really must put a few things away.

**

Panic kills

Ah, I've been there. Sometimes ignorance is bliss. I had just read a technical bulletin about the old smoke canisters we used in the early days. It had a distinctive smell and was toxic. Breathing apparatus was always worn. The bulletin declared that the smoke could also be flammable. We were on a demonstration for the public at the station and while in the base of the tower, our smoke canister suddenly ignited. Firmly in the belief that the home office was right about the smoke's flammability I decided it was time to leave. The door wouldn't open, no matter how I tried ... then I discovered that it opened the other way. I rapidly joined the smoke in vacating the building. Now, that was panic, a total inability to think clearly or rationally. It was a very useful lesson for me and was fortunately never repeated.

Even an Olympic swimmer can drown if they panic. Surprising, isn't it? But true. We must train to make our actions automatic and prepare to control our mind. Stand up and run in a fire situation and you won't even make the door. Crawl and live. 50 degrees Centigrade at floor level or 500 degrees C at ceiling level. You choose. Never stand up and run!

Another confession, I just remembered it while editing the text. I was out in remote countryside preparing an exercise for junior officers. I found a partly dismantled railway bridge alongside a road bridge over a river. I thought, 'what a great place to leave a dummy, a casualty, for them to recover.' So, armed with that idea, I walked out along a narrow girder and over the river, some distance below. I looked down and saw lower metal supporting structures – ideal for knocking yourself unconscious before being swept by the river into overhanging brambles. Already the idea for the exercise was in a shambles. Never mind placing a casualty out there, how the hell was I going to get back to my car. Frozen with fear is not an overstatement. I sure did not like it out there and the idea of turning around on that thin iron girder like some gymnast on a bar, was a step too far. The only way out was to keep going forward then take a left turn towards the brick parapet of the adjoining road bridge. Once there, the brickwork gave me confidence to not fall to an obscure and premature death. I found somewhere more convenient to leave the 'body'.

**

'So often the real truth is hidden by
what we prefer to think.'
Me

'Men occasionally stumble over the truth,
but most of them pick themselves up and hurry off
as if nothing has happened.'
Churchill

**

Gas masks from WW II

Another memory just paid a visit. It was during my first year or two in service that our leading fireman decided we should do some ladder drills. Ladder drills with a difference. Thinking back to this time, I can understand why he made us use the old war department respirators we carried on our

303

appliance. He'd served in the military during world war two and so experience must have influenced him into thinking this was something for which we should be prepared.

Well, we weren't prepared. We donned the ancient looking devices and pulled the straps tight. We were used to masks from our breathing apparatus, but air flowed freely through those. With the respirator, you had to suck like crazy in order to draw air in. I looked across at a colleague and he looked back in the same state of wonder. Wondering if the damn things were broken! They weren't, it was just how the filters worked . . . slowly! Then, as if just standing there was not enough, it was, 'slip and pitch the 30-foot ladder to the second floor of the tower. Get to work!' By the time we had pitched the ladder we had had our lesson and were gasping for breath. Such lessons are only needed once in order to carry the learning throughout life. Thank you Bill Scott. Never forgotten, always admired.

We had other stuff still carried since the war. We had an escape knife designed to cut a pilot's harness after a crash, and sear pins to insert into ejector seats to prevent accidental discharge while we were rescuing the pilot. It is amazing the amount of learning required on a myriad of subjects in order to become a useful firefighter.

**

Team building course

Two departments, operations support group, and the training centre group, were headed by one man. A man who frequently used the word 'perhaps' in general conversation. It led me to believe that one shouldn't take what he said, as being what he ever intended to happen, perhaps.

He organised at considerable expense a training weekend course on team building. We all stayed at a nice hotel and had some top trainers arrive to guide us in the right direction. That is of course their direction. I noted that in part it was also a lesson in not expecting to have what you needed but only what was available. We are back to, 'I need four people for safety,' 'sorry, make do with three.' Managing expectations. Don't have any!

Our 'perhaps' man welcomed us to the hotel, introduced the course, then said goodbye and drove away. How interesting that he didn't feel the need to be any part of the team event. And he never was, no need, he was the boss. His job was to stress everyone else, that was it, and exceedingly well paid for the privilege of doing so.

Back in training centre, myself and two others built our own team. As our desks were on one side of the room, we called it 'cooperation corner'. All too often when you needed help, advice, ideas, it took too long to receive it. I suggested that we three should always respond instantly to a request. Quite simple really, 'can you just read this for me?' 'what do you think of this as an exercise?' We would respond within minutes. Life was good in cooperation corner. Far better than the normal snail like and often denigrating or unimaginative response from the management.

**

'New shirts for old,' they cried.

In the early days at the asylum, officers wore white shirts, and the working man wore blue. I'm sure there must have been traditionally good reasons for this difference. Do you think it could be the nature of the work? One group dealing with smoke, oils and dust, all the time soaked in the sweat of strenuous labour? The essence of good firefighting was always to react quickly and calmly. Speed was our tactical friend. Once the lunatics had free range of management controls, they decided that we should all wear white shirts ... the mark of the elite. All in dazzling white.

The practicalities of keeping them clean, even after only one incident were completely lost on the decision makers. Firegrounds are not offices with convenient bathrooms and air conditioning. Do coal miners or farmers wear white shirts? Well, I wonder why not. Practicality gone out of the window, along with our prized old blue shirts that had stood the test of time. What did they think they were doing? And nothing we could do about it.

**

A couple of discipline cases

Allegedly, someone had said that a certain bloke was lazy, perhaps he was but it didn't end there as they referenced the person's colour. Someone else overheard it, even if the offended person did not. That was sufficient for whatever devious reason for the overhearing person to make an official complaint. All hell broke loose. One poor chap was suspended, and his life was a living hell, he was awake at nights and walked his village streets trying to make sense of what had happened to him. He was good bloke, and I would have said totally innocent. An investigation team of high-ranking officers was brought in from no lesser place than London. We were all interviewed in an office at HQ, and we could say nothing that would not be recorded. I know, because I asked. I had no idea who might have said what they said was said ... and I said so! After a few more questions, the scribe passed his recorded statement across to me for checking. I noted several mistakes but pointed out that one sentence was an invention and I had said nothing of the sort. The senior investigator agreed that I hadn't said it and took the paper back, crossing out the imaginary part. He then noticed that there was a spelling error and mentioned it.

'Oh,' I said, now quite aggravated by the entire time-wasting affair, 'there are lots of errors, but I didn't like to mention them.' You would have thought that they would have checked first that the recording officer was actually literate before giving him the job. Wouldn't you? We suffer too many fools gladly!

*

A retained fireman on a station, for which I was the supervisory officer, was reported by his fulltime employer for taking goods without permission from work. Basically, some defective stuff was thrown in a skip and along with a few other workers our poor chap took some home. This resulted in a disciplinary hearing at HQ. The full thing, with the Chief presiding. The defendant may not have been the brightest star in the sky, but he was a reliable, trustworthy firefighter. He was one of the station drivers and always checked who was on call before leaving the village. He made himself available at every opportunity. We needed people like him. The appliance only turned out on occasions because he was there. I said all this in his defence and was gobsmacked when the guilty verdict was announced along with his instant dismissal. Another loss caused by a gossiping nobody at, who knows, what human cost.

Hadn't they anything better to do? Wasn't there another way? 'Look here, we've heard a nasty rumour about blah blah, let's have no more of it. The next occasion could result in sanctions. Now let's get back to work serving the people, smartish.'

How different he was treated from a number of others who had committed quite serious crimes but were sheltered by the brotherhood of fellow officers. Sabbaticals, retirements and other careful planning to keep their jobs or pensions. Such unfair treatment was shocking and abhorrent to the great majority of honest caring firefighters. Their wages supporting cheats and charlatans. But nobody can change it. You can't beat the system.

**

The march on parliament 1985

The fire service protest march in London on the 6th of March 1985 was organised by our union.
I am surprised it is so difficult to discover any mention at all of this momentous event on the internet. But it did happen, I believe something like 8,000 uniformed firefighters took part, about a third of the national wholetime establishment. The

FBU organised coaches from all over to take us into London. We were dropped off not far from the Tropical medicine buildings and marched in a column for about a kilometre to the houses of parliament. The police, (officer level), treated us like animals to be herded and dealt with as undisciplined yobs. We were far from that; we were good highly disciplined and honest people united in a worthwhile cause. I had an invitation letter to meet with my member of parliament, at the time a liberal called Clement Freud ... later to be disgraced by some damning accusations of child abuse. How they call themselves, honourable, I have no idea. Perhaps it is a disease of our hierarchical system. Anyway, having gained access to the place itself, he wasn't there. They had all conveniently gone home because they were tired from talking all night. Oh dear.

**

**The truth, often never spoken,
someone has too much to lose.**

I met them all, the liars, cheats and thieves, the rotten apples spoiling the majority of kindly decent folk who gave much of themselves in honest service to others. At least one officer fabricated a route to an ill health retirement, he even told me how to do it. It was a slow process, taking up to a year, but successful. Of course, retirement seemed much easier to attain for an officer that committed a crime or was charged with one. This was a quick way out that should have cost them a pension . The offensive and offending party would miraculously be found to have an ill health issue and be retired on an enhanced pension. (Oh, sorry, allegedly, of course.) Strange that they didn't seem of ill health subsequently. Would you consider someone who sold stolen cars to be of good character? Not if you'd bought one of them, you wouldn't.

The truth is hardly ever shared.
It's just not done. It might frighten somebody or really annoy someone powerful enough to intervene. But there isn't anyone you know. No one seems to care.

I will give one fireground example only, but if you cared to look hard enough, you will find that it fits the normal experience, except you don't know that. You mustn't be upset. It is simply the way life is.
Three men died when they crashed their car. It caught fire. Now, cars and roads never cause accidents. People cause accidents, and, even that is a misnomer, as the only true accident might come from an unexpected heart attack. Everything else is negligence, ignorance, criminality or stupidity.
The police statement in the media claimed, 'Death would have been instantaneous. They wouldn't have felt a thing.'
The junior officer who attended the fire told me the truth; they would have suffered intolerably. They couldn't get out of the burning car and sheer terror had driven them to try and hide from the flames by

squeezing together as far under the dashboard into the foot well as they could. That's where their three bodies were found. It's a truth we never tell.

Perhaps that is why the roads are full of idiots.

Parked lorries do not overturn, they need to be cornered at excessive speed to achieve that. Bridges do not suddenly duck to catch out the driver of a high vehicle.

There was once a very effective fire prevention public information film on TV once, but it had to be removed as it was upsetting too many people. Wasn't that the whole point of it?

Hard to tell if the wheel wasn't there, but that is someone's car underneath the front of that lorry. Believed to be a case of overtaking at the wrong time, the driver would have had a brief opportunity to reflect on his actions and impending future.

**

The elderly

We were frequent visitors to what were called 'old people's homes', they probably have more politically correct names now, those that weren't closed down from council ownership. Privatisation was the name of the game. Did you know that at one time they considered flogging off the fire service to a private company . . . it might have been the same one that cocked up security at the London Olympics . . . not sure. We used to chat to the residents and check their buildings and procedures. At one home, we were asked to have a word with one lady, who had her own wheelchair. Whenever the alarm went off, she was in her chair and out onto the corridor. She was quicker than most, but her actions prevented anyone else from passing. In the event of a fire, she might be condemning her house mates to death. Our job? Have a word with her and explain that she needed to wait longer before exiting her room. Basically, we were saying, without saying, 'it's better you die than everyone else.' How can you choose like that? Well, I'm afraid, someone has to, life is all about decisions, preferably for the better.

Benevolent fund hampers. Every Christmas the benevolent fund sponsored a number of hampers mostly for firefighter's widows. It was a daft hamper really, poorly chosen, containing nuts that the old folk probably couldn't eat, and a couple of other unsuitable items I can't recall. The idea wasn't just to drop off the hamper and run, but to spend some time with the person, often living alone. We were out on our rounds shortly before Christmas and turned up at a small, terraced house. We rang the bell and an old lady appeared and was obviously pleased to see us. 'Fire Brigade,' we said, 'Christmas Hamper.'

'Oh, lovely, please come in.' She led us through to the little dining room at the back of the house as though long expecting our visit. We chatted with her for ages about old firefighters and the like. She was thrilled with the hamper and joined in seamlessly with our fire brigade chatter. When we left her house we left behind one very happy but completely bewildered old lady. We'd got the wrong house. She had nothing to do with the fire brigade at all. However, all was not lost, we had done a brilliant PR job for our brigade and had a nice cup of tea.

**

The welfare officer's e mails.

'I am very sorry to inform you of the death of . . . . '

Every time one comes through, I open it with dread to read the name of the lately deceased. I know how sad it will be when once close colleagues appear. Sometimes it is a just name I remember, sometimes not. But they all count, they all went to fires and the spirit of camaraderie burned within each and every one.

**

How the caring service cared for its own.

People join the Fire Service for diverse reasons, some for noble cause, some for employment, some with greater self-interest than others; the reason I stayed in the service was different from why I joined in the first place. I joined up with some people who among other things fancied the income from a shift job while they could concentrate on their main work, whether it was electrician, plumber, or running a chip shop. For all their different reasons they would still be trained the same, aspire to the same high ideals, and enjoy the camaraderie and prospect of adventure in a respected profession.

Having been to Fire Service College at Moreton a few times and witnessed the animal behaviour of some officers, I suspect their morals and ideals had long been abandoned in murky pasts. They act foolishly, thinking that their actions are secret and that they are anonymous ... they are not ... everybody who was there knows, and remembers.

I have a reason for wanting to write this. Firstly, it is like a therapy for me as I still struggle to come to terms with how I ended up retired on ill health with stress. Secondly it saddens me to see that lessons may have not been learned in how to manage personnel without destroying their minds. I can think of a number of people whose demise was not so much that of seeing terrible incidents but that of being subject to terrible management ...

this is in my opinion and based on my own experience.

Before I was 'burned out', I was full of energy, ideas, dreams and abilities but I ended up being diagnosed with PTSD and anxiety disorder.

I was consumed with guilt for not being who I had been, and no longer capable of fulfilling my duty to colleagues and public alike. Before I retired I was sought out for my knowledge, I was a trusted member of the service and able to go anywhere with impunity. The day after, I was simply a nobody who hid from fire engines.

I want to give an example of the ignorance of management in understanding how to manage people. Of course, I have been long out of the service now and I'm sure that the modern Officer is superbly equipped with the best of training and practice in dealing with stress related problems.

I digress. I had learned on the radio, of experiments carried out on mice in which some were given an electric shock regardless of their action and others were not given a shock if they passed by a barrier. Success, no matter how small was rewarded ... but the other poor devils were shocked no matter what they did. After a while of conditioning the mice were all put in a bath of water. The ones who had had the 'kinder treatment' swam to the side and got out .... The others stayed in the middle and drowned. I later discovered that this is called learned helplessness in the Psycho whatsit trade. At a staff meeting of all training, operational support staff, and appropriate senior officers I explained what I had heard. Did they understand and act on it ? No, they just laughed. There is a good word for people like that, but I shall refrain from using it. They call it learned helplessness, but I reckon that it was taught too.

**

Qualities of a Firefighter as from the tenets of the St John's Star.

Tact
Perseverance
Gallantry
Loyalty
Dexterity
Explicitness
Observation
Sympathy

What about Tactless, lazy, cowardly, treacherous, clumsy, ambiguous, short sighted and uncaring.

So, asking those senior officers, which badge would you be proud to wear? When does the caring stop and self-interest begin? When does the courage of your convictions have to be put aside to gain promotion? When does tact mean you were looking the other way? It goes on.

After you retire for a while, it is amazing what you learn, even beyond some of the unsavoury facts that you already knew and witnessed yourself.

No one publishes them, as protecting the good name of the service is everything. We all know what has gone on in the past. There are bad people across the world and the fire service is not exempt from their intrusions. Meanwhile, too many good people were lost due to mental health issues – all of them quite avoidable. Can't you see?

Cause and effect ... an inescapable law.

Pictures of my twenty-year medal and my service belt line .. which holds the better memories?

'Stop message from a retired Station Officer, 'Stop for lost dreams, no further assistance required. Mobile to final address, no longer available, over.' The end.

**

Do not seek to follow in the footsteps of the wise, seek what they sought.

**

Farewell

Derek, myself, Eddie and Rod.
To me, they were heroes three.
Much of what I valued most in my career came from
the inspiration and guidance from them.
Photo taken at a farewell party organised for me.
Something I was afraid to attend, filled with doubts
and guilt, until I met the truly fine people who had
come to say goodbye. For that, I can't thank those
present enough for the memory.

**

I leave you now with the gift of story, one that
characterises the soul's desire of all firefighters.

Suspicion.

*An Edwardian tale of adversity and courage
during hard times.*

The oil lamp hanging from the beam swung wildly
on its hook and the flame flickered desperately as
the old Inn door opened to the wild night,
hurriedly ushering in a wind battered visitor.

Old Seth the village mole-catcher pushed his body
hard against the door to close it tight and secure
the latch. 'By God,' he said, 'that be devilish windy
this night it be.'

'No moles to be caught tonight then Seth,' joked
the burly innkeeper, pouring him a tankard of ale
from the big jug.

'If I know ee moles, they'll take advantage of this
bad weather and be all over his Lordship's lawn by
teatime come morning's night,' muttered Seth and,
like a pack of hunting wolves, the wind around the
ill-fitting windows howled in accord.

Seth shuffled his old boots across the sawdust floor
and sat in his favourite chair. Nearby, were four
men, strangers they were, and though next the
inglenook wood fire they still wore their great
coats with collars turned up. Caps, the mark of a
working man, covered their heads, and their boots
looked the worse for wear. Occasionally a gust of
wind forced smoke down the chimney, oblivious,
the men talked on, absorbed deeply in their
secretive liaison.

Seth's friendly greeting, 'Eenin to ee gents,' was
largely ignored, only one man, the larger of the

four thickset men, grunted back, 'An' yerself squire,' then quickly turned his face away for the work in hand.

'Ah well,' mused Seth, 'obviously strangers, not a local accent, seemed sort of ... well, not sure really ... anyway, strangers they were and mean looking ones at that ... wouldn't want to meet them on a dark night.'

Seth supped his ale in a peace of his own making. Now Old Seth might have been getting long in the tooth but there was nothing wrong with his hearing. Some said he could hear moles moving underground – some even said he talked to them. Though some would also say, 'old wives' tales mostly – mostly'.

Seth didn't hear all that was being said, he just caught bits of the conversation; 'gotta get money soon', 'counting on us back 'ome', 'take our chances when we can I say', 'what about the rich geezer's big house down the road', 'shh, not so loud.' .....

William, the big innkeeper, came close and placed a callused and powerful hand on old Seth's shoulder, the hand of part time village blacksmith, 'See 'ere old Seth, I'm putting ee another fine log on the fire to keep ee warm and happy. Now don't ee forget that kindness when ee next sees his Lordship's woodsmen.'

'Ar, to be certain, there's always plenty of useful men about at his Lordship's,' Seth said, loud enough so as the four men could not fail to hear. At the same time, he spoke to William with his eyes, indicating his distrust of the strangers with a sideways look and an enquiring expression.

Seth went back to the bar with William on the excuse of obtaining more ale, but as they huddled over the bar it was other things that occupied their minds. For some half hour they chewed over what they should do about their suspicions but before they could decide, the Inn door burst open. Standing in the open doorway, with no intention of closing it, was one of the Earl's gardeners, 'Big trouble up at the House and we need help quick.'

By now he has the attention of everyone in the Inn, ... including the four strangers who are now all looking straight at the gardener with earnest intent.

'What's wrong, my friend?' asked William, peering past the wind flickered lantern.

'Fire, Fire, ... stables on fire ... the horses trapped ... his Lordship is begging for help to save his horses ..... will you come?'

'We're on our way old chap, we're on our way.' As William threw on his rough old coat, he shouted at the strangers, 'I'm sorry lads, but us have got to go, ye'll have to leave the Inn, I'm sorry.'

The men stood quickly in unison.

'Nah worries guv, we're coming wiv yer,' shouted back the big fellow. With heavy chairs pushed back like they were nothing, they all reached the door together and then out into the dark night. William grabbed two lanterns and they set off hurriedly on the gravelled mile to the manor house.

Soon they were close enough to smell the fire and hear the horses' tortured cries of fear.

It was a scene of total chaos at the stables; stone built of two stories, the stalls being on the ground floor and storage above, wooden beams, floors and walls everywhere. Straw and winter hay was well alight with ever thickening dark yellow smoke, servants ran and shouted, even the kitchen girls were there ... not that any could do much to help.

William, Seth and the strangers found his Lordship by the closed main door to the stables. Though beside himself with pain for an impending and horrific death of his beloved horses, he managed to explain, 'Fire, started in loft, burnt through floor, far end of stables, the end where we usually get in, horses down this end but we can't open doors from here ... only from inside. The way through is barred by fallen beams and fire .. My God, just listen to those poor creatures. What can we do?'

'If it can be done sir, it will be done, ee have my word on it,' William said, with more than a note of fervent promise in his voice. And with that, the six moved as one to the burning end of the building. There was a small bucket chain from the well in use, but to little avail, they would never extinguish such flames, the only hope was to open the doors from the inside and save the horses, for the barn was already condemned to a fiery hell. William and the big fellow looked through the door together, much of the fire was still on the upper floors, tiles could be heard breaking on the floor above as parts of the roof failed, in front of them, a few feet in, was some smoking, water damped straw and a muddle of fallen timbers, some of them huge beams of oak.

William turned to the big fellow and said, 'Look, I can't do this on my own, but I reckon it's clear past this point and I feel I can open they far doors an let they horses out. Can you, ... will you ... help I past yon beams?'

'Count on us squire, what we've been through in life, we ain't afraid.' Pulling their collars higher and wrapping some old hemp sacking around their hands and arms they entered through the doorway to hell.

'Seth,' shouted William, 'get ee to the main door, tell his Lordship to be ready for they horses. And with that, he disappeared choking into the yellow grey smoke.

Seth glanced in horror as five men disappeared from sight as if forever. He hoped upon hope that the building would stand long enough for William to do his work, he then, quick as old bones would let him, went to find his Lordship.

Strong as William was, the beam that barred his way was beyond his strength, as he crouched low to gain some fresher breath for one last attempt, he heard the big fellow shout, 'go for it mate, we can't hold it up much longer.' William saw through stinging, tear blinded, eyes the four strangers had lifted the beam enough for him to get through. He didn't waste a second, for with every second he was getting weaker and more confused. As he'd hoped, it was cleaner air further down the stables, he followed the stall fronts on the left to the great doorway and, fumbling with shaking but powerful

324

hands, he found the bolts and locking bar that freed the door to open. With an almighty shove, fresh air rushed in to greet him as the heavy door swung open. As good as his word Seth was prepared, along with the stable boys and his Lordship, to guide the frenzied horses away to safety. It was going well, despite the horses being panicked and kicking out, they were all released safe to a corner field. 'Let it burn now, let it burn,' called his Lordship, 'don't risk yourselves anymore, my beautiful horses are safe, God bless you all for your help.' His composure soon regained, his Lordship ordered the kitchen staff to prepare refreshments for his helpers, and for everyone to stand back from the now collapsing building. The roof caved in first and carried the first floor down with it, the falling twisting beams levered the stone walls as they fell, and it was all but over for the old stables. It was a smoke laden and sweat smelly throng that gathered in the great kitchen, his Lordship mingled with his servants like they were bosom friends, the like of which was never seen before nor since. 'William, Seth, good friends that you are, heroes both that you are, you will know my gratitude in the days to come, you can be sure of that,' beamed his Lordship, who had been liberal with the port as much as with his thanks.

Seth drew his Lordship aside, 'what of they four strangers, milord, I'm not seeing they since the fire, perhaps they need a watching sir.'

'Nay Seth, good men all, they saved the day for us with their strength and camaraderie, without their bravery our noble William could not have prevailed against the odds as he did. Good men all, simple working folk, iron ore miners walking their way to Northamptonshire for the promise of work to feed their families. I've had the butler sort them out some fresh clothes ... not burnt ones, eh? ... Here they come now. Here lads, here, come join us for a meal,' he called.

They sat about the great pine table, food and drink a plenty, there they sat, his Lordship, the Mole-catcher, the black-smith and ... no, not four strangers anymore, just four good men that could look any other in the eye and tell their tale of heroism.

But I doubt they ever would, so here, I have done it for them.

**

There could have been more to tell, there was more, there's a limit though, and we've arrived.

Printed in Great Britain
by Amazon